FAITH AND FREEDOM BASIC READERS

This Is Our Parish

REVISED EDITION

Sister M. Marguerite, S.N.D., M.A.

Sister M. Bernarda, C.PP.S., PH.D.

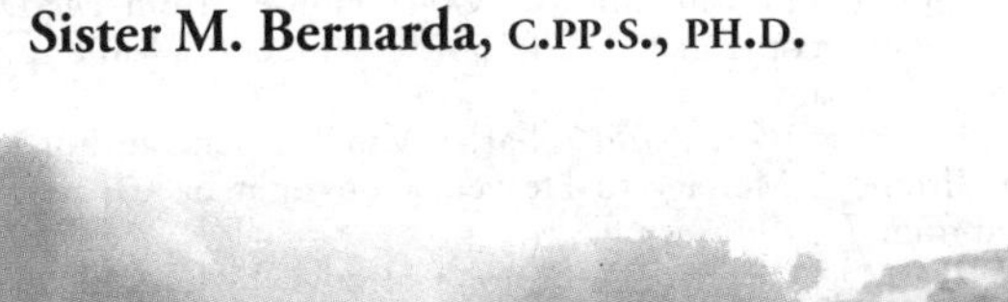

GINN AND COMPANY

Boston • New York • Chicago • Atlanta

Dallas • Palo Alto • Toronto

ACKNOWLEDGMENTS

Grateful acknowledgment is made to the following authors and publishers for permission to use copyrighted material:

Appleton-Century-Crofts, Inc., for "Book Houses" by Annie Fellows Johnston, from *St. Nicholas Magazine,* copyright 1919, The Century Company, reprinted by permission of the publishers Appleton-Century-Crofts, Inc.

E. P. Dutton & Co., Inc., for "Jump or Jiggle" by Evelyn Beyer, from *Another Here and Now Story Book by* Lucy Sprague Mitchell, copyright 1937, by E. P. Dutton & Co., Inc., reprinted by permission of the publishers.

J. B. Lippincott Company for "God's House," from *For Days and Days* by Annette Wynne, copyright 1919, 1947 by Annette Wynne, published by J. B. Lippincott Company.

The American Weekly and Charles Van Deusen, author, for "A Letter to Heaven," from "A Message to Heaven," copyright by Charles Van Deusen and reprinted from *The American Weekly.*

Child Life Magazine for "The Apron Calendar" by Lucy Elder, copyright 1955.

Children's Playmate Magazine, Inc., for "Around-the-World Playmates" by Daisy D. Stephenson.

Educational Publishing Corporation for "The Laughingest Family," reprinted from *Grade Teacher,* by permission of the publishers.

Girl Scouts of the U.S.A., for "Finding the Brownies," based on their adap-tation of the original story by Juliana H. Ewing, reprinted in *Leader's Guide to the Brownie Scout Program.*

Mary A. Goulding for "Peggy and Ginger."

Highlights for Children, Inc., for "The Cat That Went to the Palace" by Martha Johnson, from *Children's Activities,* April, 1947; also for "The Blue Umbrella Surprise," from "Don't Open the Blue Umbrella" by Gertrude Keller Mack, from *Children's Activities,* April, 1957, by permission of Highlights for Children, Inc., Columbus, Ohio, owner of the copyright.

Jack and Jill and the following authors for selections adapted and reprinted by special permission of and copyright by The Curtis Publishing Company. Ivy O. Eastwick for "The King of the Fishes," from "Bianca and the King of the Fishes," © 1958; Marjorie Hopkins for "Lippity-Lop Cleaning Company," © 1959; Helen M. Horne for the dramatization of "The Bossy Fairy," © 1950; Paul Tulien for "The Zipper Jacket Triplets," from "The Martin Triplets," © 1958.

Lilian Moore for "Big Bear and the Pond," originally published in *Humpty Dumpty's Magazine.*

Ilo Orleans for "Bless This House," from his book *This Wonderful Day,* copyright 1958.

Parents' Institute, Inc., for "The Shoes of Mr. Van Jan" by Wilbur Wheaton; "The Elephant That Liked Ice Cream" by Sally Jarvis; "Corky's Surprise," from "Serena's Surprise" by Martha B. Stiles, all copyright 1957 and originally published in *Humpty Dumpty's Magazine.*

Margaret O. Slicer for "The Hat with Cherries on It."

FAITH AND FREEDOM

NIHIL OBSTAT:

Rev. Gerard Sloyan, S.T.L., PH.D., CENSOR DEPUTATUS

IMPRIMATUR:

† Patrick A. O'Boyle, D.D., ARCHBISHOP OF WASHINGTON

Washington, January 15, 1962

COMMISSION ON AMERICAN CITIZENSHIP
THE CATHOLIC UNIVERSITY OF AMERICA

Rt. Rev. Msgr. William J. McDonald, *President of the Commission*

Rt. Rev. Msgr. Joseph A. Gorham, *Director*

Katherine Rankin, *Editorial Consultant*

Sister Mary Lenore, O.P, *Curriculum Consultant*

PUBLISHED FOR THE CATHOLIC UNIVERSITY OF AMERICA PRESS
WASHINGTON, D.C.

Contents

Parish Friends

Learning to Help Others

Laughing Together

Parish Feast Days

The Parish Library

Good Times Together

Illustrations by Carl Bobertz, Hazel Hoecker, Albert Jousset, Margot Locke, Forrest Orr, Ray Quigley, Gilbert Riswold, Catherine Scholz.

Parish Friends

Fairlands, Here We Come

The Fay family had always lived in the city. Now they were going to live in a town.

Mr. Fay had a new job in Fairlands. So the Fay family was going to live there.

The three children, James, Michael, and Karen, laughed and talked as the car took them to their new home.

"I see a church," cried Michael, as they came near the town.

"And I see a school with a cross on it," cried Karen.

"Is that where we will go to church and to school?" James asked.

"Yes," said Daddy to the children. "That is Saint Peter's Catholic Church and school."

"Is it the only Catholic church and school in Fairlands?" Michael asked.

Daddy laughed and said, "Oh my, no. There are two more Catholic churches and schools. They are in other parts of the town."

"But we will live in this part of the town," Mother told the children. "So we will be in Saint Peter's parish."

“What is a parish?” Karen asked. “How can we be in a parish?”

“That just means that we live in a parish,” James tried to tell his sister.

“No, it means more than that,” said Daddy. “The parish is like one big family. It is made up of all the people who go to the same church.

“In a parish the people pray together, work together, and have good times together.”

"I can't wait to see what the school is like," said James.

Karen laughed and said, "And I want to know who will teach us."

Daddy smiled at the children. "We will soon find out about all of these things," he said.

"Everything is new for us," said James. "We are in a new town. We will have a new home, a new church, a new school, and new friends."

"Fairlands, here we come!" cried Michael.

Strangers in the House

"I thought this would be a new house," said James.

"It will look like new after we work on it," said Daddy.

"It looks like a kind of spooky place to me," said Michael. "I guess no one has lived here for a long time."

"Here we come, spooky house," laughed Karen. "Are you happy to see us?"

"Now get busy," said Mother to the children. "Each one of you has a job. Let's see how fast we can fix up some of the rooms."

All day long the family worked. When evening came, they were very tired.

By nine o'clock, the house was dark. Everyone was in bed.

All at once Karen heard something. It seemed to come from the wall.

Karen sat up in bed. She was too frightened to move.

"Bump-bump-bump!" Karen heard the sound again.

She jumped out of bed and turned on the light. She put her ear to the wall. "Bump-bump-bump!" she heard.

Just then the door of her room opened. And in came her two brothers.

"There must be spooks in this house," Michael said to his sister. "We heard strange sounds coming from the walls."

"So did I," said Karen in surprise. "What do you think it is?"

"Spooks!" cried James. "Real spooks! Let's call Daddy."

The three children went to Mother and Daddy's room. When they got there, Mother was up. She was looking outside.

"Where is Daddy?" Michael asked.

"Down in the living room," Mother answered. "Why are you out of bed?"

"We were frightened, Mother," said Karen. "We think there are spooks in this house."

"We all heard strange sounds coming from the walls," said James.

Just then Daddy came into the room. "Well, what does this mean?" he asked when he saw the three children.

"The children heard the strange sounds, too," said Mother.

"I can't find a thing to be frightened about," Daddy told the family. "So let's go back to bed and sleep. In the morning, we can take a better look."

The next morning, Daddy went up on the roof. He put something into the chimney.

Out of the chimney scampered four little squirrels.

“There go the spooks!” laughed Daddy.

That day he fixed the chimney so that the squirrels could not get back into it.

And after that there were no more spooky sounds in the house.

Meeting New Friends

One day Daddy asked, "Would you like to go to meet some new friends?"

"We would love to do that," said Karen in a happy way.

Michael did not want to go. He only wanted to see his old friends.

He had no one to play with in the new town. Oh, how he wished that he could go back to the city!

But he smiled, put on his jacket, and went with the family. They walked a little way and saw a beautiful Catholic church and school.

The Fay family went into the church to pray to Our Lord. Michael began to feel better. Our Lord was always his friend.

When they came out of the church, Daddy said, "The priests of our new parish live in that white house. Let's go to see them."

Father Denis opened the door.

"How do you do, Father," said Mr. Fay. "We are the Fay family. We are new in your parish."

"I am happy to know that you will be in this parish," the priest said. "My name is Father Denis."

Then he shook hands with each one of the family. He seemed to hold Michael's hand a long time.

"What a happy smile he has!" Michael thought. "He seems like an old friend."

Father Denis called the pastor. He wanted the family to meet him.

"This is our pastor, Father Burns," he said when the other priest came in.

"We want our children to come to the parish school," Mr. Fay said. "Will you have room for them?"

"Yes," said the pastor. "We shall be happy to have the Fays in Saint Peter's School. Let me show you the school.

"School starts next week," he said. "So some of the teachers are working in their rooms today."

First, the children met Miss Ball.

"This is Karen Fay, a new girl for your room," Father Burns told her.

"I shall be happy to have you in my room, Karen," Miss Ball said and gave a big smile.

"Don't any Sisters teach in this school?" James asked.

"Yes, there are four Sisters," said Father Burns. "And there are four teachers who are not Sisters."

"Who will be my teacher?" Michael asked.

"You will be in Sister Bernadette's room. Mrs. Woods will teach James," said the pastor.

Michael liked Sister Bernadette as soon as he saw her. She seemed so kind.

"Well, I have one more friend," he thought and smiled a little more.

Father Burns showed the family the rest of the school. Then he told the boys something.

"You will make new friends very fast in our town," he said. "We have Cub Scouts here."

Now Michael was very happy. He had been in the Cub Scouts in his old school. He knew that was a good place to make many friends.

"Oh, we want to be in the Cub Scouts at Saint Peter's," he said at once.

The Fay family thanked Father Burns and said good-by to him.

On the way home, Michael said a little prayer. He thanked God for his new town, his new parish, the new friends he had made, and the new friends he would find.

The Zipper Jacket Triplets

The Martin twins lived near the Fay family. Their names were Betty and Bob.

One of the things the twins liked to do was to play with their father's old zipper jacket.

Bob would put his right arm into the right arm of the jacket. And Betty would put her arm into the other arm of the jacket. Then they would zip it up.

Now, Mr. Martin was a very big man. So the jacket was just right for the twins.

One day, when the twins came home from school, they found a letter. It was from Mother, and this is what it said:

> Daddy and I had to go downtown. We will be back before dinner. Go to Grandmother's house until we come to get you.
>
> Love,
> Mother
>
> PS. Help yourself to milk and cookies.

"Shall we go right away?" Betty asked her brother.

"Let's have milk and cookies first," said Bob.

After Bob ate his after-school lunch, he ran to get the zipper jacket.

"Let's wear it to Grandmother's house," he said.

Bob ran out into the yard. He put his arm into the jacket. Then he put the jacket around a tree.

“No room for you!” he called to his sister when she came out.

“Oh, yes, there is!” laughed Betty. She pulled the zipper down. Then she put her arm into the jacket and pulled the zipper up again.

“Look!” she cried. “There’s room for all three of us. Why don’t we go to Grandmother’s like this?”

“Don’t be silly,” answered her brother. “How do you think we would ever get the tree out of the ground?”

He reached up to pull the zipper down. It would not move.

"I can get it," said Betty.

She reached up. She pulled and pulled. But the zipper would not move.

"Now what will we do?" asked Bob. "The neighbors are away. We will have to stay here until Mother and Daddy come home."

"Oh, someone will see us before that," said Betty. "Look, there comes Mr. Fay in his car."

"Mr. Fay! Mr. Fay'" called the twins.

Mr. Fay called hello and went on. He did not know that the children needed help.

The twins began to feel very sad. What would they ever do if someone did not come soon to help them?

Soon a friend of Daddy's came by. He took pictures for the newspaper.

When the twins saw him, they cried, "Mr. Star, please come and help us!"

Mr. Star smiled when he saw the children. "First, let me take your picture," he said. "This will make a good story for the newspaper."

After the picture was taken, Mr. Star asked the twins how old they were. "We are seven," answered Bob.

"And this tree is seven, too," said Betty. "It is just as old as we are."

"Well, then you are triplets!" laughed Mr. Star.

On Sunday, Mother and Daddy saw the picture in the newspaper. They read how the Martin twins had become triplets.

After that, the Martin family called the tree their "triplet tree." And their friends called Betty and Bob the "zipper jacket triplets."

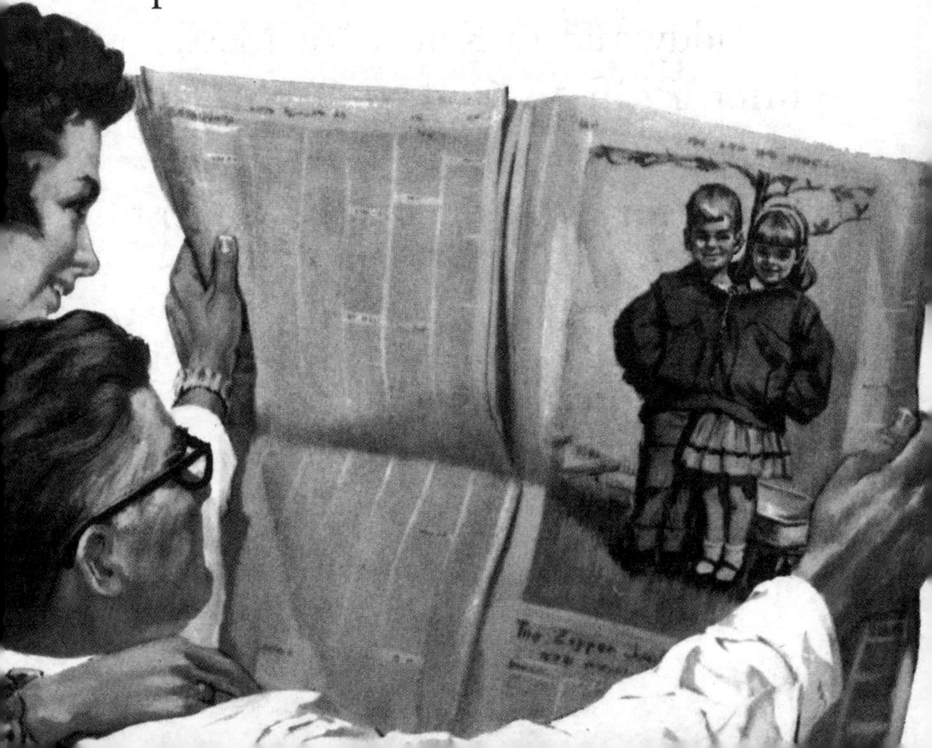

Gifts for God

On the first day of school, the three Fay children were up with the birds.

"We shall all go to the seven o'clock Mass together this morning," Daddy said.

"But the Mass is so long for me," said Karen. "I get tired because I can't read the big words in my prayer book. I just have to look at the altar all the time."

"That's because you don't know what the Mass is," said James.

Daddy said to Karen, "At Mass, we offer a gift to God, Our Father in heaven."

"But what kind of gift can we offer to God?" Karen wanted to know.

"At Mass, we offer Jesus, the Son of God, to His Father in heaven," said Mother.

"I don't see how we can give Jesus to His own Father," said Michael.

"This is the way we do it," Daddy said. "First we offer bread and wine.

"Then the priest takes the bread in his hands and says what Our Lord said, 'This is My Body.'

"The bread then becomes the Body of Jesus. It looks the same, but now something great has happened to it. It is the Body of Jesus.

"Next the priest takes the wine. He says the same thing that Our Lord said at the Last Supper, This is My Blood."

"The wine then becomes the Blood of Jesus. It looks just as it did before, but it is now the Blood of Jesus.

"Jesus Himself is now on the altar. And we can offer Him as our gift to God, the Father."

The three children walked into the church with Mother and Daddy. They saw many other people there, too.

All had come to offer their gift to God in the Mass.

Mother and Daddy prayed the Mass prayers with the priest and the other people. Michael and James prayed with them, too.

Karen looked at the pictures in her small prayer book.

Then she stopped and said this prayer: "Dear God, I love You very much. In this holy Mass, I am going to offer a big gift to You. I am going to give Jesus to You. You love Jesus very much, dear God. So You will love my gift."

Father Burns offered the bread to God. Then he offered the wine.

Before long, the altar boy began to ring a small bell. There was not another sound in the church. The priest took the bread in his hands and said, "This is My Body."

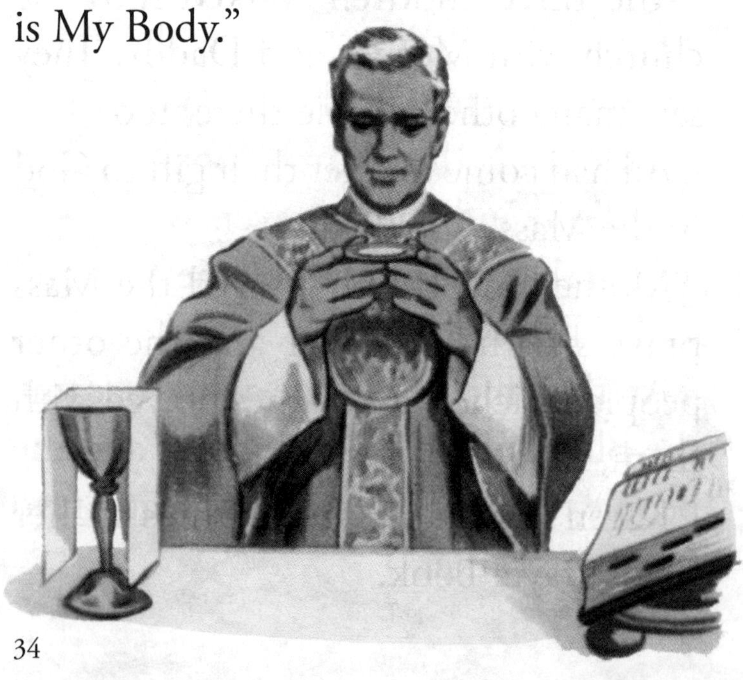

At that very moment, the bread became the great gift of Jesus' Body.

Father Burns was holding the Body of Jesus up for all the people to see. Everyone in the church looked up at Our Lord and said a prayer.

After that, the priest took the wine and said, "This is My Blood."

At that moment, the wine became the Blood of Christ. The priest and the people together offered this great gift to God, the Father.

One Turn Too Many

Michael's Turn

"I have the ball!" said one of the boys in Michael's room, as the children ran out into the schoolyard.

Father Denis was waiting for the boys.

He liked to play ball with them. He could throw well. He could catch well. And he could run very fast.

One boy after another had a turn to throw the ball. Then someone called, "Your turn, Michael!"

Michael was holding the ball. He was going to throw it when the bell started ringing.

Michael did not hear the bell, or maybe he just wanted to have his turn to throw.

Michael let the ball go! But no one was there to catch it. The other boys had started walking into school.

Zip-bang! The ball went right into a window in the meeting room.

Michael was frightened. He looked around. No one saw me throw that ball," he thought to himself. "Maybe no one will know what happened."

Michael ran to catch up with the other children. He walked into the schoolroom with them.

He took out his book and opened it. But all he could think of was the window.

Would Sister Bernadette ask, "Who broke the window?"

Maybe Jim, the workman, would come and tell Sister about it.

Would Father Burns, the pastor, come to ask who had broken the window?

"If someone asks about the window," thought Michael, "I will not tell that I broke it."

When it was time for lunch, Michael tried his best to get out of the room as fast as he could. But Sister Bernadette stopped him at the door.

"Michael," she said, "do you know who broke the window in the meeting room?"

Michael looked at Sister and said, "No, Sister. I didn't even know that the window was broken."

Sister Bernadette looked at Michael as if she knew something. Then she told him to run home and eat his lunch.

James and Karen were waiting for Michael. As soon as he came out, the three children began to run up the street.

The three children did not go far when Michael stopped.

"I have to go back to school," he said. "Please tell Mother that I will be a little late for lunch."

"What did you forget?" James asked.

"Oh, just something," Michael said, as he ran off down the street again.

Michael did not go into the school. He went over to the church. For a moment he stood in the back of the church and looked all around.

Then he walked up near the altar. He looked up at the altar and said a prayer.

"Dear Jesus," he said. "I am sorry for what I told Sister about the window. Please help me to own up now. I love You, Jesus, and I want to do what is right."

As Michael went by the priests' house, he saw Father Denis.

"Hello, there, Michael!" called the priest.

"Father, I want to tell you something," Michael said. "I am the one who broke the window in school this morning."

"Does Sister Bernadette know that you did it?" the priest asked.

"No, Father," answered the boy. "Sister asked me about it, but I didn't want her to know that I did it. So I told her that I didn't know anything about it. Now I am sorry."

Father Denis looked at Michael. "What do you think you should do about it?" he asked.

"I think I should pay for the window," said Michael.

"Yes, you can do that," answered the priest. He waited for Michael to say something more.

"I think I should tell Sister Bernadette what I did," said Michael.

"Yes, that's it," smiled the priest. "Run and tell her now. Sister will feel better about it, and so will you."

"Thank you, Father," said the small boy. And he ran to see his teacher.

"I am glad that you came to tell me about the window," Sister said to Michael after he had talked to her. "I know that Our Lord and His Blessed Mother are glad, too."

She smiled at him. Then she said, "Run home now and get some lunch. Maybe you can help Mr. Jim put some new glass in the window."

"Oh, I will be glad to do that," Michael said and away he ran. Now he was hungry!

The Blue Umbrella Surprise

Mandy Muggins was a friend of Karen's. She lived on the same street. Mandy and her brother Peter went to Saint Peter's School.

One day Peter Muggins went running down the street. He ran and ran until he was very tired. Then he sat down to rest.

The little brown dog that was with him sat down, too.

Francis Horn, the newsboy, saw Peter. "What's all the running about?" he asked.

"It's about my sister Mandy," said Peter. "I have to find her so she will not open the blue umbrella."

"Oh, is that all!" said Francis Horn. And he went on his way.

Peter was resting when a policeman came by.

"Have you seen my sister Mandy Muggins?" Peter asked.

The policeman thought for a moment. "Yes, I think I did," he answered.

"Was it raining when you saw her?" Peter asked.

"Well, it could have been," said the policeman. "It's been raining on and off all morning. Why do you ask?"

"Because if it rains, she will open the blue umbrella," answered Peter. "And if it does not rain, she will not."

"Well, that sounds all right to me," said the policeman. "If I see Mandy, I will tell her that you are looking for her."

Peter and his little brown dog began running again until they met a man in a truck.

"Good morning," said Peter. "Have you seen my sister Mandy?"

The man in the truck was tired and said, "I have not seen anyone's sister. Why don't you ask the man in the store? He sees more people than I do."

So Peter and his dog went into the candy store.

"Good morning," Peter said to the store man. "Have you seen my sister Mandy Muggins?"

"Yes, she was in here just a moment ago," said the man.

"Was it raining?" Peter asked.

The man thought for a moment. Then he said, "Yes, I think it was. It's been raining on and off all morning."

Peter looked sad. "Did Mandy have a blue umbrella with her?" he asked.

"Yes, she did," answered the man.

Peter began to talk faster. "Was the umbrella opened?" he asked.

"Of course not," laughed the man. "Who ever opens an umbrella indoors?"

At that very moment, Mandy Muggins went by the store. She had the blue umbrella, and she was scampering up the street. Soon it began to rain.

Peter Muggins ran after his sister just as fast as he could go. "Don't open that umbrella, Mandy!" he called. "I've been looking for you all morning to tell you not to open the umbrella."

Mandy stopped and turned around. "How silly!" she cried. "What's an umbrella for? It's raining."

Just then Mandy began to open the blue umbrella. Something small and green came out of it.

"Oh, Peter! What is that?" she cried.

"That's what I've been trying to tell you about," said Peter. "It's my new pet turtle. I put him in the umbrella last night so he would not get away."

"Well, who would ever think of finding a turtle in an umbrella!" said Mandy.

By that time, Peter had his pet turtle. "You can open the umbrella all you want now," he told his sister as they walked home together.

Blessing the Homes

One morning after Mass, Mr. Fay went to see Father Burns.

"Our home here in Fairlands has not yet been blessed, Father," he said. "Do you think you could come over and bless it one of these days?"

"I shall be happy to do that," said the kind pastor. "There are some other new families in the parish who have asked for the same thing.

"Why don't you all get together and have the blessing next Sunday?"

Mr. Fay looked at Father Burns. "I don't think I know what you mean, Father," he said.

The priest smiled. "In this parish, the people like to do things together," he said. "Sometimes the Catholic families on near-by streets have their homes blessed on the same day."

The priest went on. "The families go from one home to the next. They all pray together in each home. Then in the last place, they have supper together."

"That sounds great to me," said Mr. Fay. "We would be happy to be with our neighbors for the blessing. Maybe they can all have supper at our house, too."

"Yes, they could do that," said Father Burns. "But every family will help with the supper. Each one will bring something to eat."

At four o'clock on Sunday afternoon, the Fay family walked over to the first house to be blessed.

It was a small white house where the King family lived. They had three children, but they were all too little to go to school.

Father Burns and the other families were there, too.

James, Michael, and Karen met a girl about as big as Karen. Her name was Mary Rock. Her brother was about as old as James. His name was Billy.

After all the people had met one another, the blessing began.

From the King's house, the priest and people went up the street to another house. The Rock family lived there.

The people prayed with Father Burns as he blessed the home.

After that, Doctor Gabriel's home was blessed.

At last the priest and people reached the Fay family's house. Father Burns blessed it.

Then the families had supper together.

Of course, there were all kinds of surprises! Big cakes and small cakes. Homemade bread, pies and buns, chicken, and other good things.

At supper, James, Michael, and Karen sat near Billy Rock and his sister Mary.

"Why don't you come to our school?" they asked their new friends.

"Daddy tried to get us in there, but it was too late," answered Billy. "There was no more room."

“We just moved here last week,” said his sister.

“We will go to Saint Peter’s every Saturday,” said Billy. “The Sisters will teach us about God. Then maybe later on we can get into the school for good.”

That evening, after all the people had said good-by, the Fay family sat down in the living room. They were tired, but happy.

“Now our house is a holy place,” said Karen.

“Yes,” said Daddy. “And we must all try to keep it like that.”

Bless This House

God, bless this house,
Its roof, its walls,
Its friendly rooms,
Its stairs and halls.
I pray Thee, God,
To all who live
Within this house
Thy blessings give.
Protect them from
The winds that blow,
From rain and storm,
From winter's snow.
And in this house
May never cease
Thy gifts of joy,
Of love, of peace!

Ilo Orleans

Learning to Help Others

Jesus Helps Some Friends

The children were learning about the things Our Lord did when He lived in this world. Father Burns told them this story.

One day, Jesus and His holy Mother were asked to a wedding feast.

Our Lord loved His friends. He liked to be with them. He liked to make them happy. So He and Mother Mary went to the wedding.

Many other people were there, too.

As the people were eating, the Mother of Jesus saw that the wine was almost gone. She saw, too, that some people at the wedding feast had not had any yet.

Now Mary knew that the man and lady who were having the wedding feast were poor. She thought they would be very sad if some of their friends had to do without wine.

So Mary went to Jesus and said, "They have no more wine."

Our Lord looked at His holy Mother. He knew what she wanted Him to do.

He said, "It is not yet time to let the people know that I am the Son of God."

Mother Mary only smiled. Her Son was good and kind. She knew He would help His friends.

Mary said to the waiters, "Do whatever Jesus tells you to do."

Now, in the room there were six big water jars.

Jesus called the waiters. "Fill these jars with water," He said.

"Now take some to the head waiter," He told the waiters.

How surprised the head waiter was! "Why, this is the best wine I have ever had," he said.

Jesus had changed the water into wine because His holy Mother asked Him to.

Jesus and Mary love us. They want to help us, as they helped their friends at the wedding feast.

Mary will ask Jesus to help us if we pray to her.

Our Lord loves His Mother so much that He will do all she asks of Him.

The Little Shoes

Here is a story which Father Denis told the Cub Scouts one day. It is about a little boy and some parish helpers.

In a far-off country, there once lived a little boy. His parents were very poor. Sometimes there was not even food in the house for all of the family.

One cold morning, when the boy was putting on his patched clothes and old cloak, his mother walked into the room. She looked at his poor little shoes.

"These shoes are too bad for you to wear out of the house," she said. "You will catch cold."

"Mother, please let me go this morning," said the boy. "I told the Blessed Mother that I would go to Mass and Holy Communion every day."

The boy's mother knew how much her son loved Jesus and His Mother Mary. So she said, "Well, you may go today, but it will be the last time.

"I do not know how I can buy new shoes for you. We have only a little food in the house to eat."

After Mass, the boy went over to the Blessed Mother's altar. He looked up at the beautiful statue.

"Dear Mary," he said, "I cannot come to Mass tomorrow. I want to come, but I have no shoes to wear. See, these are very old. My mother does not want me out in the cold with them on. So, dear Mother Mary, if you want me to come, please help me."

As the boy looked up at the statue, Our Blessed Mother seemed to smile down at him. Then he got up and started home.

Just as the boy was walking out of the door, he met the kind pastor.

The priest smiled. "I see that you come to Mass and Holy Communion every day," he said to the child.

"But I have to stop coming now," said the boy, and he began to cry.

“Why can’t you come any more?” asked the priest.

“Because I have no shoes to wear,” answered the child in a sad voice. And he showed the priest his old shoes.

“That’s too bad,” said the priest. “But maybe I can do something about your shoes.”

The kind pastor took the child to the priests’ house. There in one of the rooms stood a box of all kinds of shoes.

There were big shoes and little shoes and even shoes for babies.

“Where did you get all these shoes, Father?” the boy asked.

"We have many good men in this parish who like to help others," answered the priest. "They bring shoes and clothes for people who need them."

The pastor looked and looked in the box. He wanted to find the right kind of shoes for the child. Soon he found some.

"Oh, these are just right!" cried the child. "How nice and warm they feel!"

"Wear them home," the priest said. "Our Blessed Lady must have wanted you to have these shoes."

The little boy thanked the kind pastor. Then he ran home as fast as he could.

The child's mother was very happy to see the nice warm shoes.

"Now you can go to Mass and Holy Communion every day," she said.

Then she gave the boy some bread and milk. She gave him an apple, too.

The child looked at the apple. He liked apples very much.

"I will not eat this," he said to himself. "I shall offer it to the Christ Child. It is all I have to give Him."

Once again the boy went to the church. There he offered his gift to the Child Jesus in His Mother's arms.

The boy's love for Jesus and His Mother grew day after day. Soon he began to pray the Rosary every day before the same beautiful statue.

And when he grew up to be a man, he began to write beautiful songs and prayers about our Blessed Mother.

Finding the Brownies

Grandfather Needs Help

Karen heard this story at one of her first Brownie meetings.

"What are children good for anyway?" said the little old grandfather as he worked.

"Children are a blessing," answered his wife. "That is what I was always taught."

She was an old woman who could no longer do her own housework.

"Well, just look at the two in this house," said Grandfather. "Tom plays all day. Mary would step over a thing before picking it up."

"But they are beautiful and kind," said his wife.

"That does not make them good for anything," answered Grandfather. "They don't like to work. And that's that."

At that moment, Tom and Mary came into the house. They had been playing outside, and their shoes were not clean.

"I have cleaned this house once today," Grandfather told the children. "And I am not going to clean it again."

"What makes Grandfather so cross today?" Tom asked.

"He is tired," answered Grandmother. "He needs someone to help him. You children don't do a thing for him."

"But how can we help?" Mary asked.

Grandmother did not answer, but she told the children a story about a brownie. This brownie was a little elf.

"When I was a little girl, a brownie used to come and do all the work at night," Grandmother said.

"The brownie lived in our house for a long time without anyone seeing him. Then one night, one of the maids saw him. His clothes were very old.

“The maid, of course, was sorry for the brownie. So the very next day, she made a nice warm cap and jacket for him.

“That night, the brownie put on his new clothes. He danced right out of the door. And he never came back again.”

“Where did he go, Grandmother?” Mary wanted to know.

“What happened to him?” asked Tom.

“No one but the wise old owl knows that,” said Grandmother.

“Who is the wise old owl?” Mary asked.

“Oh, oh, I don’t know,” Grandmother laughed. “Long ago, my mother used to talk about the old owl. Sometimes she did not know the answer to something. Then she would say, ‘Only the wise old owl knows.’”

“There’s an owl in our oak tree,” Mary thought. “Maybe that owl knows where the brownies are.”

Mary Learns Something

That night, Mary saw the old owl sitting in the oak tree.

Mary went to bed, but she thought about the old owl for a long time. Then she had a dream. In the dream she was talking to the owl.

"Could you please tell me where to find the brownies?" she asked.

"Oo-hoo, oo-hoo! I know two!" answered the old owl.

"Where do they live?" Mary asked.

"In your own house," said the owl.

Mary looked surprised. "How could they?" she asked. "They never work."

"They don't like work," said the owl.

"Maybe they don't know how to work," said Mary. "Maybe no one ever taught them how. I would if I could find them."

"Oo-hoo, oo-hoo! Would you?" asked the owl. "Then go down to the pond. Turn around three times and say this:

'Twist me, turn me, show me the elf.
I looked in the water and saw_____.'

Then think of the last word."

Mary ran off to the pond. She turned around three times and said this:

"Twist me, turn me, show me the elf.
I looked in the water and saw_____."

Mary looked into the water.

"Let's see," she said to herself. "Jeff, belf, welf. Self! Oh, dear, could that be it? I did see myself in the water."

She ran back to the oak tree and told the owl what had happened.

"That's right," said the owl. "You are a brownie. All children are brownies."

Then the owl told Mary how she and her brother could help Grandfather and Grandmother each night.

"Don't tell anyone but Tom," he told Mary. "Don't let anyone see you."

Mary told Tom about her dream. From that night on, things were different.

The house was always clean when the old man and woman got up each morning. They did not know what to think.

"I guess a brownie must be somewhere in this house," Grandmother said.

"You had better not look for him, Grandmother," laughed Mary. "You might frighten him away again."

One day, Grandfather made a little red cap and jacket for the elf. What a surprise he had the next morning!

Tom came dancing down wearing the little jacket and cap.

Grandfather was going to punish Tom. But Mary told him what she and Tom had been doing.

"At last, we have found real brownies," laughed Grandmother.

Grandfather made a little coat and cap for Mary. And never again did he ask, "What are children good for?"

Surprises in the Woods

Karen was happy as she and Marie walked to their Brownie meeting together. Today the Brownies were going to find surprises in the woods.

Karen walked into the Brownie room and took Jean's hand. Up went her other hand. This was her new Brownie way of saying hello. Then Karen said hello to all the other girls in the same way.

Before the eight girls started on their trip to the woods, Marie said, "I made a picture for our Brownie book."

"It is a good picture, Marie," said Mrs. Brooks, the Brownie helper. "It shows the signs that we learned at our last meeting.

"I put some signs like this in the woods this morning. So now we can go, but you must do what the signs tell you if you want to find some surprises."

Away the girls went to the woods. They found some rock signs right away.

They walked to the left. Then they walked to the right. At last, they found a letter from Mrs. Brooks.

It said, "Walk nine steps to the right and find something small but beautiful."

The Brownies saw a flower. It was very small, but it did not seem pretty.

Jean looked at the flower again and said in a quiet voice, "It is just a little flower, but look at its pretty colors."

The Brownies looked at the flower again and said, "Oh, it is beautiful!"

Then they found more rock signs and a letter from Mrs. Brooks. It told them to look in an oak tree to find an animal.

Up in the tree there was a squirrel in its nest. The girls knew that they might frighten it. So they were very quiet.

All at once, they heard something beside the tree. This was a real surprise—even for Mrs. Brooks.

It was a beautiful bird. It tried to fly, but it could only move a little. Its leg was broken, and its wing was hurt.

The Brownies took the bird back to their meeting place. Mrs. Brooks helped the eight girls to fix the bird's leg. Then they put the bird into a big box.

"Brownies should do a good turn every day," said Mrs. Brooks. "They should do something without wanting someone to pay them back.

"We have done a good turn for one of God's little animals today."

Karen laughed and said, "And there is no way that a bird can pay us back."

Each day, the girls gave the bird some food. Before long, the bird started to get better. It even began to move its wing.

One day the Brownies looked into the box. Their beautiful bird was gone! Then they saw the bird flying about the room.

The girls and Mrs. Brooks took the bird back to the woods. It flew up into a tree.

The Brownies were quiet as the bird sang a beautiful song. It seemed to thank the Brownies for their help.

You were not right, Karen," laughed Jean. "A bird can pay us back for a good turn. It is paying us now with its beautiful song."

A New Kind of Club

One afternoon, the boys and girls in Miss Ball's room talked about a mission club.

"I wish we had a good name for our mission club," said Tom.

"So do I," said Betty Jean. "Maybe we can think of a good name."

"All right, you may all think of a good name at home this evening," said Miss Ball. "Tomorrow we will see which one we like best."

That evening, the Fay family tried to help Karen think of a good name for the mission club.

"I know a fine name," laughed Daddy. "Why not call it the Three W's Club?"

"What do the three W's mean?" asked James.

"Who can guess?" asked Daddy. James guessed that the three W's stood for We Will Work.

"That would be a good name," laughed Daddy. "But it is not the right one."

Everyone guessed, but no one was right. At last Mother said, "Maybe we had better give up, and Daddy might tell us what the three W's mean."

"All right," smiled Mr. Fay. "The three W's mean Wee Willing Workers."

"Oh, that's a good name," cried Karen. "Do you think Miss Ball will like it?"

The next morning, when Miss Ball walked into the room, the children were busy talking about their mission club.

"Karen has the best name!" the children told their teacher.

"My daddy thought of it," said Karen. "He said we could call our club the Three W's Club."

"But we can't guess what the three W's are," said another little girl.

Then Karen told Miss Ball and the children that the three W's stood for Wee Willing Workers.

"That's a good name," cried the boys and girls.

"It's the best name yet," said Timmy.

David looked at Miss Ball and said, "We have a good name for our Club. But what kind of work are we going to do?"

Then Miss Ball told the children about the work of the missionaries. She said, "In some far-away places, babies are found in the streets. Their parents sometimes put them there because they can't afford them."

She said some babies are taken to missionaries because the parents are too poor to take care of them. So the adopt them.

"Do they really adopt the babies?" Denis asked.

"Yes, they adopt the babies," Miss Ball said. "And, of course, the missionaries are glad to adopt them. They want to teach them about God."

“Do you think we could help the missionaries adopt a baby if we had some money?” asked one of the boys.

“Yes, that would be a fine thing to do for the missionaries,” answered Miss Ball.

“My mother saves stamps for the missions,” said a girl. She told me that stamps are almost as good as money.”

“That’s right,” smiled the children’s teacher. “We could save stamps from old letters.”

“Let’s make a bank for our money and a box for the stamps,” said Denis.

"I know a good way to make a bank," said Mary Ann. "We can get a milk bottle and dress it up like a baby doll. When we look at the doll, we will think of the baby we want to adopt."

"And we will put our money into the milk-bottle baby!" laughed Timmy.

"That will be fun!" cried the children. "Let's dress one bottle like a boy doll and the other bottle like a girl doll."

Before long the Wee Willing Workers had two doll-baby banks made from milk bottles. They had two boxes for stamps, too.

Making Easter Baskets

The Strange Little Hen

Joan Green was in Room Three at Saint Peter's School. She and the other children in that room were making Easter baskets for the sick children.

One afternoon, when Joan came home, she found a box with her name on it.

"May I please open the box right away, Mother?" she cried.

"Yes, you may open it if you wish," her mother answered.

Joan worked fast as she pulled the paper off. "What can it be?" she thought.

When Joan opened the box, her eyes grew bright.

"Oh, Mother! Come and see what Uncle Bill gave me," she called. "Here are candy eggs and rabbits and little candy chicks."

Joan picked up a little toy hen, and a red candy egg came out. "What is this?" she said in a surprised voice.

She shook the toy hen, and a brown candy egg came out.

"Why, candy eggs are falling out of this little hen!" she said.

Each time anyone picked up the toy hen, a different colored egg came out.

Joan tried to see how many candy eggs she could get. Then she thought of her Easter basket for the children at Fairlands Hospital.

"Shall I keep this little toy hen, or shall I put it in my basket for the hospital?" she asked herself.

"I guess I had better keep it. After all, it's my gift," she thought.

But a little voice inside her seemed to say, "Give it to one of the sick children in the hospital."

For a moment, Joan was almost willing to give up her little hen. Then she thought, "No, Uncle Bill might not want me to give his gift away."

That evening, Mother helped Joan color eggs to put into her basket for the hospital. They made a nest and placed the eggs in it.

"Would you like to put in one or two of your candy rabbits?" Mother asked.

The little girl was glad that Mother did not say anything about the little hen.

So she answered, "Oh, yes, Mother, let's put in two candy rabbits."

Joan took the rabbits out of the box and put them into the nest.

Joan's Gift

The next day, all the boys and girls in Joan's room took their baskets to school for the sick children.

Joan began to feel a little strange as she put hers with the others. She thought that she had not been as kind as she should have been.

Joan went home for lunch, but she didn't seem very hungry.

"What's wrong, Joan?" Mother asked. "You are not eating anything."

Then Joan told Mother what she was thinking.

Mother knew how Joan was feeling. She said, "You don't have to give away the little hen. But if the Christ Child were in the hospital, I am sure you would want to give it to Him."

"Oh, yes," cried Joan. "I would be very happy to give something to Jesus."

"Every boy and girl in this world is one of God's children," said Mother. "When you do something for one of them, you do it for Christ Himself."

"Do you think that God would even want my funny toy hen, Mother?" Joan asked.

"If Our Lord were one of those sick children in the hospital, I am sure He would," answered Mother.

"I think He would, too," said Joan.

Joan ran all the way to school. She took with her the toy hen that Uncle Bill had sent. No one was in the schoolroom when she got there. So Joan put her toy hen into the basket.

All at once, Joan was very happy. She had given away something that she had wanted to keep.

It was her own gift for God. And no one saw her do it—no one but the good God Who knows everything.

He must have been pleased with His little girl.

Around-the-World Playmates

The world is one big neighborhood;
Good friends have you and I
Who share the same wide tossing
seas,
The same blue arching sky.

The children of the Orient,
Brazil or Italy,
The little folks of every clime
Are much like you and me.

So let us make a magic ring,
And friendly greetings call;
The world is one big neighborhood,
And we are playmates all!

Daisy D. Stephenson

Laughing Together

Fun Day at Saint Peter's

On the day after Easter, Saint Peter's School had a day called Fun Day. The children in each room did something funny. And all of the other children in the school were there to see it.

They had funny shows, did tricks, told stories, or sang songs. The child who did the funniest or best thing got a prize.

Most of the boys and girls thought of what they would do for Fun Day weeks and weeks before Easter time.

There was one little girl in Karen's room who was very sad about Fun Day. Her name was Maria. She had come from a country far away.

Maria had not been in our country very long. She did not know how to speak like the other children. Most of the time, she did not know what the other children were saying.

Maria did not know about Fun Day. But Karen told her all about it.

"I can't speak right," Maria thought. "So I can't tell a story or read. I don't know any tricks."

Maria was sad because she could not think of anything to do.

"How I wish I could go back to my own country!" Maria said to Karen.

"But you will love this country, Maria," Karen said.

That same evening, Maria told her family about Fun Day. She even asked her parents if she could stay home from school when it came.

"Why, Maria," said her father. "I know just the thing for you to do. It is something very different."

Maria looked at her father.

"What about a dance?" he said. "You and Willy can do a dance together. You know, the kind we used to do back in the old country."

Maria thought for a moment. Then she asked, "But where will we get the music? No one around here can play that kind of music for us."

"I will take care of that," said her father. "I can play the music, and you children will dance."

Fun Day came at last. Maria was frightened when the children in her room began their show.

Maria heard the boys and girls clap when funny stories were told. This made her feel even more frightened.

"They will never, never clap for me," Maria thought. "I am sure they will only laugh at me."

Maria started to run out of the back door when Sister Joan saw her. "Come, Maria," she said. "We are all waiting to see you dance."

Maria's father began to play. Willy was ready. So he and Maria began to dance.

At first the music was slow. Then faster and faster it went. And faster and faster went the feet of the two little dancers. They twisted and turned.

The other children in the school clapped and clapped and clapped.

Maria was happy because the other children liked the dance.

She and her brother twisted and turned around and around.

The children clapped louder than ever. "Maria! Willy! More, more!" they cried. They all wanted the little girl and boy to dance some more.

When it was time for the prizes, Maria and Willy were called first. How surprised Maria was to get the first prize!

Guess what it was? Our country's flag and a beautiful big picture book about our country—Maria and Willy's new home.

Lippity-Lop Cleaning Company

Here are some of the stories which the children told or read on Fun Day. They were all prize stories.

Mrs. Chipmunk got up one morning and looked out of the door. "This is a nice day for house cleaning," she said.

So she began to clean her little house in the old rock wall.

Now, Mrs. Chipmunk always had her house nice and clean. She had a place for everything. She even had her seeds stored in an old ice-cream box.

She put the box of seeds out in the yard because she wanted to clean her house.

Mrs. Chipmunk was so busy that she did not hear Mr. Rabbit coming by.

Mr. Rabbit owned the Lippity-Lop Cleaning Company. It was his job to go around and pick up all the trash that the animals left in their yards.

Today Mr. Rabbit saw the box of seeds near Mrs. Chipmunk's door.

"My, Mrs. Chipmunk has so much trash today," he said to himself.

He picked up the box and put it into his truck. Then he started riding off.

When Mrs. Chipmunk had finished her work, she went out to get the box of seeds. Of course, they were not there.

"Now what has happened to that box of seeds?" she said in a half-loud voice.

"You mean that old box that was near your door?" said a voice over her head.

It was Mr. Crow sitting up in the oak tree.

"Yes, I do," answered Mrs. Chipmunk looking up at the crow.

"The Lippity-Lop Cleaning Company. took it away," laughed the crow.

The crow had seen Mr. Rabbit going down the road with the chipmunk's seeds.

"And you didn't stop him!" cried Mrs. Chipmunk.

"Maybe you can catch him if you hurry," the crow told Mrs. Chipmunk.

So away scampered Mrs. Chipmunk as fast as she could go.

On her way, Mrs. Chipmunk met Mr. Fox. "Have you seen Mr. Rabbit from the Lippity-Lop Cleaning Company?" she asked.

"Yes, he went through the woods eight or nine minutes ago," answered Mr. Fox. "Maybe he has finished his work by this time and has gone home."

Mrs. Chipmunk ran to Mr. Rabbit's house, but she saw no sign of the rabbit. So Mrs. Chipmunk went into his house to wait until he came home.

There she saw an old bag of leaves. "My, Mr. Rabbit has so much trash in his house," she said.

She pulled the bag outside to be picked up by the cleaning company.

After she had cleaned the house, she sat down and went to sleep.

As Mrs. Chipmunk was sleeping, Mr. Rabbit came to his own house. Without thinking, he picked up the bag of leaves.

"There is more trash around today than ever before," he said to himself. And he put the bag of leaves into his truck.

At that minute, Mrs. Chipmunk got up. She looked outside and saw the truck going up the road with the bag of leaves.

"Well, well, Mr. Rabbit has picked up his own trash," she laughed. "I must catch him and find out about my seeds."

"Mr. Rabbit! Mr. Rabbit!" she called as she ran after the truck. "Did you pick up a box of seeds at my house today?"

"Sure, I did," answered the rabbit.

"Well, please take that box right back to my house. You had no right to pick it up," said Mrs. Chipmunk.

"Sorry, lady," said Mr. Rabbit. "But whatever gets into my truck goes into the fire."

"Now, don't be so mean," said Mrs. Chipmunk. "After all, I cleaned your house today. I even put your trash out to be picked up. See, there it is. It is that old bag of leaves."

Mr. Rabbit jumped up. "That bag of leaves is my bed," he cried. "I picked it up because I thought it was just some more trash."

"Well, well," laughed Mrs. Chipmunk, "Your bed will have to go into the fire, too. That's what happens to whatever gets into your truck, you know."

Mr. Rabbit sat down to think. Then he said, "All right, for this one time we shall change things around. I'll take your box of seeds back to your house. And I'll take my bed back, too."

"Good!" said Mrs. Chipmunk. And she jumped up into the truck and rode back to her house in the Lippity-Lop Cleaning Company's truck.

Big Bear and the Pond

Big Bear was getting old. He took more time looking for good places to sleep than for food to eat.

One very hot day, Big Bear was walking through the woods. To his surprise, he came to a pond near some fir trees.

"How nice and quiet it is here," said Big Bear. "And it's not hot at all."

It was just the right place. So Big Bear began to go there every day.

Now, that was fine for Big Bear. But it was not fine for all the little animals.

The pond was theirs. They came to the pond for a drink or to find their food. To them, the bear was a robber.

"What shall we do?" a squirrel asked the chipmunks.

"What shall we do?" a bunny asked the rabbits.

At last one chipmunk said, "We must have a meeting."

So that evening, they had a meeting. Everyone came, even the smallest squirrel and his best friend, the smallest chipmunk.

"How can we make Big Bear go away from our pond?" the animals asked. They talked and talked and talked, but no one seemed to know what to do. Not even the oldest chipmunk.

Not even the oldest squirrel.

Not even the oldest rabbit.

The next morning Smallest Squirrel and his friend, Smallest Chipmunk, played a new game. They called it "meeting."

They put their noses together and talked about the big bear.

"Maybe we can frighten him away from the pond," said Smallest Squirrel.

"Frighten him? A big bear like that!" said Smallest Chipmunk.

"Maybe an elephant would frighten him," said Smallest Squirrel.

"Yes, an elephant would frighten us, too," said Smallest Chipmunk.

"They say that Big Bear is very, very big," said Smallest Squirrel. "Let's go through the woods to the pond and take a good look at him."

So the two little animals scampered up a tree and looked down at Big Bear. My, how big he was!

Just then something happened. A long green worm started to fall out of the tree. It landed on Big Bear's nose.

Big Bear opened one sleepy eye. He began to laugh, "Tee-hee, tee-hee, tee-hee."

The worm began moving on the bear's nose. Big Bear laughed some more.

Big Bear moved his nose so fast that he made the worm fall to the ground. Then he went back to sleep again.

"Big Bear does not like to be tickled," said Smallest Squirrel.

"No, he does not," said the chipmunk. The two little animals got very busy. Cut-cut-cut-cut! Soon they had cut down part of a tree with some leaves on it.

They began to tickle the bear's nose.

Big Bear opened one sleepy eye. He began to laugh, "Tee-hee, tee-hee, tee-hee."

The two little animals tickled and tickled. They tickled his feet. They tickled and tickled.

"Oh, please stop," laughed Big Bear.

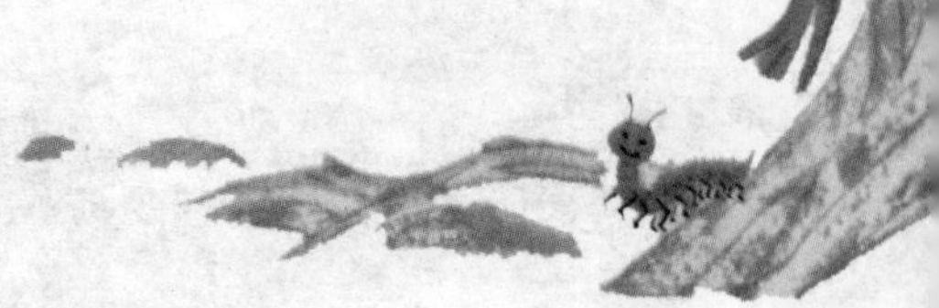

But Smallest Squirrel and Smallest Chipmunk did not stop.

At last the bear could take it no longer. He jumped up and ran off as fast as he could.

"I don't think he will ever come back to this pond," laughed the squirrel.

"Now our friends have a place to drink and to swim and to look for food."

The happy little animals scampered home to tell the good news. That evening they had the best supper they ever had.

The Elephant That Liked Ice Cream

"When can I have a part in the circus?" asked Jingo, the baby elephant. "All the other animals do tricks."

"Oh, Jingo, you are too small yet," said his mother. "You can't even hold up one of your legs without falling over."

"Oh, look here, Mother," said Jingo.

He put his one leg up. But then he put the other one up. Bang! He sat down on the ground.

"You see, Jingo, you are too little to do tricks," said his mother. "But if you are good, I'll let you walk in the parade."

So the baby elephant could only dream of a real part in the circus.

The next day all the animals got ready for the circus parade.

"Now, whatever you do, don't let go of my tail," Mother Elephant told Jingo. "Follow me all the way to the big ring in the circus."

The band started to play. First came the horses. Then came the clowns dancing to the music. One even had a monkey.

"Here come the elephants!" the children cried.

Each elephant was holding on to the tail of the one next to him. The very last one was Jingo, the smallest elephant of all. He was holding his mother's tail.

Just then Jingo saw something. It was the ice-cream man!

Now there was not a thing in the world that Jingo liked more than ice cream.

He didn't remember to hold on to his mother's tail. He didn't remember what his mother had told him. He didn't even remember that he was in the parade.

Jingo let his mother's tail go and ran after the ice-cream man.

"Look at that funny little elephant!" cried the children. "He is as funny as the clowns."

Jingo fished into the man's bag and pulled out some ice cream.

The ice-cream man did not see Jingo.

He walked on. Jingo went on eating ice cream. He ate more and more ice cream. Soon the man's bag began to feel light. "What has happened to all my ice cream?" he cried in a surprised voice. The children laughed. "Turn around and see what is following you," they said.

When the man saw the elephant, he became frightened. He let the bag fall and ran.

Jingo looked around. He was all alone.

At that very minute, a clown came out to see why the children were laughing so hard. He saw the baby elephant.

"Oh, you could work with me," the clown said to Jingo. "We could make the children laugh and have a good time."

The next day, the clown dressed up like an ice-cream man. Jingo followed him, eating ice cream out of his bag.

The boys and girls laughed and laughed. Jingo was happy now. At last he had a real part in a circus.

The Shoes of Mr. Van Jan

Just as Mr. Van Jan sat down in his big chair to rest, his wife said, "Why, Carl, where are your shoes?"

"Shoes?" asked Mr. Van Jan. "What shoes?"

"Your own shoes, of course," said his wife. "You had them on when you went to our neighbor's house."

"Oh!" said Mr. Van Jan. "My shoes! I must have left them at the pond."

"Carl!" said his wife in a cross voice. "Have you lost the only shoes you own? You must find them at once."

Mr. Van Jan put on his little cap and coat and went out into the dark.

At last he reached the pond. He looked and looked for the lost shoes.

He was ready to give up when a tiny voice called out, "Stop that! You are stepping on me."

Mr. Van Jan looked down in surprise. There sat a little elf near the water.

But the thing that surprised Mr. Van Jan most was the elf's feet. They were almost as long as the tiny elf was tall.

What was more, the elf was trying to put on some shoes—Mr. Van Jan's shoes.

"What are you doing with my shoes?" cried Mr. Van Jan.

The little elf laughed. "Can't you see what I am doing?" he asked.

"How would you like to give me these shoes for two little white stones?" the elf asked Mr. Van Jan.

"White stones!" cried Mr. Van Jan. "What good would stones be to me? My yard is filled with stones."

"But these stones will give you and your wife each a wish," said the elf.

Mr. Van Jan picked up the stones and started home. "Remember, only one wish on each stone," the elf called.

When Mr. Van Jan reached home, he said to his wife, "See what I have."

Mrs. Van Jan looked at Mr. Van Jan's feet. "Where are your shoes?" she asked in a cross voice.

Mr. Van Jan started to tell his wife about the elf and the stones.

"Oh, dear!" said Mrs. Van Jan. "I wish you had shoes big enough to sleep in. Then maybe you would remember to keep them on your feet."

At that very minute, there was a sound at the door. Mr. and Mrs. Van Jan went to see who was there. When they looked out, they had more than a surprise.

There were two very, very big shoes. Just what Mrs. Van Jan had wished for! Shoes big enough to sleep in!

"Where did those shoes come from?" asked Mrs. Van Jan.

Then Mr. Van Jan told her all about the two stones and the two wishes.

"Why didn't you tell me before?" said the cross wife. "I could have wished for something better than shoes."

Mr. Van Jan began to feel very cross.

Then Mrs. Van Jan said, "Well, this never would have happened if you had remembered to bring your shoes home."

By this time Mr. Van Jan was very unhappy. "Shoes, shoes, shoes!" he cried. "I wish this house were filled with shoes. Then we would never—" He stopped.

But it was too late. He had made a wish.

The room was almost filled with shoes. The Van Jans ran out of the house. Soon the house was filled with shoes.

When the Van Jans looked through the window, their eyes grew bright. They could see all kinds of shoes—little ones and big ones.

"Now what will we do?" cried Mrs. Van Jan.

That night they went to sleep in the big shoes that were in the yard.

The next day, Mr. Van Jan made a small shoe store, and he began to sell shoes. Soon he had all the money he needed.

Mrs. Van Jan made him keep fifty of the shoes. "You may forget your own shoes again someday," she laughed. "So we will keep enough on hand."

Corky's Surprise

Corky, the duck, had everything she wanted. She had a nice barn in which to sleep. She had a pond in which to swim. And she always had good food to eat.

Every morning, the goats went out to find their breakfast.

The chickens and their baby chicks went into the barnyard for food.

The rooster crowed, "Cock-a-doodle-do!" A boy came to the barn to milk the cow. Then Corky knew it was time to walk into the yard and over to the pond.

Better than anything, Corky liked to swim in her pond.

One very cold morning Corky got up late. The boy had milked the cow long before Corky got up.

Corky put on her shawl and walked over to the pond.

But something was wrong! Something hard was on top of the pond.

Corky ran back to the barnyard. One of the goats saw her running and asked, "What's wrong, Corky?"

The rooster crowed, "What's wrong?"

"Oh, oh, oh!" cried Corky. "Something bad has happened to my pond."

"Something ba-a-a-d?" asked the goats.

"What, what, what?" asked the hens.

Rags, the dog, heard the animals and came to see what was wrong.

"Something is on my pond," Corky said.

Rags ran to the pond.

"Why, that is ice, Corky," he said.

"Can you take it off?" asked the duck.

"It will only come off when it gets warm," answered the dog. "If we could make it hot, the ice would go away."

"What will I ever do if I can't swim?" asked the duck in a sad little voice.

"Maybe the cow can help," said the dog.

So the dog and the duck walked over to the cow. "Bossy, you are a big animal," Rags said. "If you would go out and sit on the ice, it would crack. Then Corky could swim."

"I could never do that," said Bossy. "I might catch cold."

So Rags asked the goats if they would walk on the ice so it would crack.

"Oh, we could never do that," said the goats. "We may hurt our legs."

"I will go to the house," said Rags. "Maybe the farmer will know what to do."

Rags ran into the house. Soon he came back with two bright things.

"What are those bright things?" Corky asked when she saw them.

"These are ice skates!" answered the dog. "When you put them on your feet, you can skate right on top of the ice."

"Can I carry the skates?" Corky asked.

"Sure, here they are," said Rags.

As Corky and Rags walked through the yard, all the chickens and all the other animals wanted to know what they had.

"Ice skates, of course," answered the little duck. "All you have to do is to put them on your feet. Then you can swim right on top of the ice."

The goats, the chickens, the rooster, and the cow all stayed at the pond to see what would happen.

Corky put on her skates and got on the ice. It was not at all like swimming. One foot went one way, and the other foot went the other way.

Clang! Corky sat down so hard that she saw stars.

"Baa-a-a," laughed the goats. "Cluck-cluck," laughed the hens.

The rooster laughed and even Bossy, the cow, had a big smile on her face.

Corky got up and tried over and over again. She was ready to give up, but just then she found that she could skate.

"Why, this is great!" she cried. "It is more fun than swimming!"

She skated three times this way. Then she twisted herself around and skated three times the other way. She was as happy and proud as a duck can be.

Corky skated every day after that until the warm days came again. She was sorry when the ice began to crack and she had to put her ice skates away.

The Cat That Went to the Palace

Once upon a time, a very pretty kitten lived with a little old woman in a small house.

The house was in the woods where it was dark and cold. But inside the little house it was always warm and bright.

People did not know how this could be. The woman owned only one tiny light!

But the little old woman always said, “It is my beautiful kitten that makes my house so bright and warm.”

When the kitten grew up, everyone said that he had become a beautiful cat. So the cat became very, very proud.

In the little old woman's house there also lived a tiny elf. No one but the cat knew that the elf was there.

One day, when the cat was talking to the elf, he said, "I am far too beautiful to live in a place like this. I should live in the king's palace."

"What are you thinking of doing?" the elf asked.

"I am thinking of going away," answered the cat. "I'm sure the king would be most happy to have a beautiful cat like me."

"You will be sorry," said the elf. "You know what you have here, but you don't know what you will have in the palace."

But just the same, the cat ran away from his house in the woods.

And, of course, the little old woman was very, very unhappy to be alone.

The elf could not talk to people. So he could not tell the little old woman what had happened.

The cat got to the palace, and the king saw him. He said, "Now, that is what I call a beautiful cat. We must keep him here in the palace."

The cat, of course, liked to hear that. He became prouder than ever. "At last I am where I should be," he said to himself.

"Don't be so sure about that," said a tiny voice. "If I could get out of here, I would go this very minute."

It was another little yellow elf that lived in the palace.

"What silly talk!" said the cat.

"Just wait and see," said the elf.

The next morning, a maid came to see the cat. She put a band of ribbon with little bells on it on the cat. The bells would ring every time the cat moved.

"Now you look like a palace cat," said the king when he saw the cat.

That night the proud cat could not sleep. The ribbon hurt him. He told the elf all about it.

"Just wait," said the elf. "Wait and see what will happen next."

Every day the king thought of something more to put on the cat. One day it was a new coat. Then it was a ribbon for his tail. He also had little green boots made for the cat's feet.

Day after day, the cat grew more and more unhappy. "I can't move with all these things on me," he told the elf.

Then one day the king thought of something different.

"This cat has lived here in the palace for nine days and has not had a bath," he said to the maid. "Fix a pot of hot water and give the cat a good bath."

A bath! A bath for a cat! This was more than the cat could take. So when the maid started getting the hot bath water ready, the cat jumped out of the window.

That evening, he found his way back to the little old woman's house. How happy she was to see her beautiful cat again!

After that, the cat never liked to hear anyone say that he was beautiful.

Jump or Jiggle

Frogs jump
Caterpillars hump

Worms wiggle
Bugs jiggle

Rabbits hop
Horses clop

Snakes slide
Sea gulls glide

Mice creep
Deer leap

Puppies bounce
Kittens pounce

Lions stalk—
But—
I walk!

Evelyn Beyer

Parish Feast Days

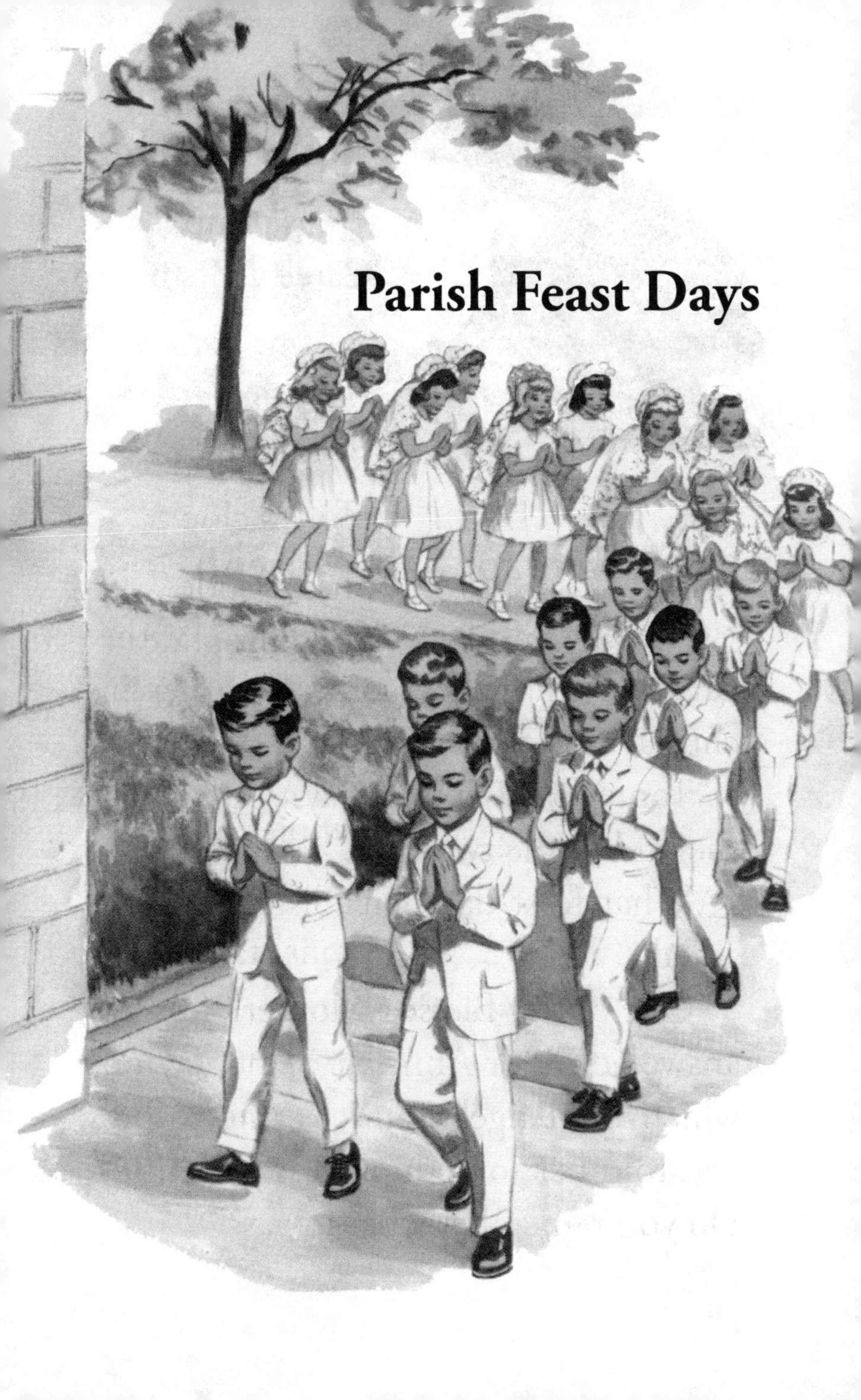

Flowers for Saint Joseph

One day, Sister Ann told two of the Brownies that they could help her in church after school.

"Tomorrow is a feast day, you know," she said to the two girls.

"What feast day is it, Sister?" Marie asked.

"One of our Blessed Mother's feasts," answered Sister Ann. "It is the day on which the Angel Gabriel came to her and told her something very beautiful. Do you remember what it was?"

"I do," said Betty. "The angel told Mary that God wanted her to be the mother of Jesus."

Sister took a box of beautiful flowers to the church.

"You may put these flowers in vases for our Blessed Mother's statue," she said.

"Are you going to put all the flowers by the statue of Mary?" Betty asked. "I think Saint Joseph should have some."

Sister Ann smiled. "I am sure that would make good Saint Joseph very happy," she said. "We will also put a vase of flowers by his statue."

The Brownies went into the work room. Then things began to go wrong.

They found two vases for the flowers. One was large, and the other was small.

Marie picked up the large vase. She was going to take it to Sister Ann for the Blessed Mother's altar. But Betty stopped her.

"That's for Saint Joseph," said the excited little girl.

"Oh, no, Betty," said Marie. "The small vase is for Saint Joseph."

"He is going to have that big one," said Betty. She reached for the vase so fast that it fell and broke.

Sister came to see what had happened. Two frightened little girls with red faces were crying.

"Betty did it!" cried Marie in an excited voice.

"Yes, Sister, I did," said Betty. "I wanted the big vase for Saint Joseph, and Marie would not let me have it."

"Do you think Saint Joseph is happy to see things like this?" Sister asked. "Now we have no vase for him."

"I'm sorry, Sister," said Betty. "I have some money in my bank at home. Maybe Mother will let me use it to buy a new vase. I will run home and ask her right now."

Soon Betty was back. A tall man was with her. He had a big box in his arms.

"Mr. Gates wants to give Saint Joseph a vase, too," said Betty.

"Yes, Sister," smiled Mr. Gates. "This little girl came into my store to buy a vase. I would like to give a gift to Saint Joseph, too. So here are two vases for his statue."

"It's a good thing I went to Mr. Gates' store," Betty told Sister Ann, "because I had only fifty cents."

"Only fifty cents!" said Sister Ann in surprise. "But you can't buy a vase like this one for fifty cents."

Mr. Gates smiled at Sister. "Let's forget about the money," he said. "These vases are a gift for good Saint Joseph."

Before Marie and Betty went home, they went to Saint Joseph's statue to say a little prayer together.

Then the girls went to the Blessed Mother's statue.

Betty said, "Dear Blessed Mother, I am sorry that I was mean and cross today. But I am sure you are glad that Saint Joseph has some flowers, too."

Peter the Fisherman

The feast of Saint Peter was a big day at Saint Peter's Parish. On that day Father Burns, the pastor, offered the Mass to God for the people of the parish.

Each year the children were told something about Saint Peter. Here is one of the stories they liked best.

One morning Our Lord was walking along the lake.

He saw two fishermen in their boat and called to them. "Come, follow Me, and I will make you fishers of men," He said.

The two men got out of their boat and went with Jesus. He asked them to be His friends and helpers. So these men became the first apostles of Jesus.

They were brothers. One was named Simon, but Jesus changed his name to Peter. Sometimes He called him Simon Peter.

Peter loved Our Lord very, very much. He always wanted to be with Him.

One evening, Our Lord told His apostles to go to the other side of the lake. He wanted to be alone and pray to His Father in heaven.

The apostles said good-by to Jesus and left Him alone for the night.

The next morning, the apostles tried to get back to land. But it started raining hard. The wind blew the boat around like a toy. The apostles were frightened.

All at once they saw something strange upon the water.

They heard Someone say, "It is I. Do not be frightened."

Peter stood up and cried, "Lord, if it is You, tell me to come to You upon the waters."

And Jesus said, "Come."

Peter jumped out of the boat. He began to walk over the top of the water.

For a little while, Peter thought nothing at all of what he was doing. Then he thought, "What if I should go down into this water!"

At that very moment, Peter started going down, down, down. He cried out in a loud voice, “Lord, save me!”

Jesus put out His hand and helped Peter. He asked, “Why are you frightened? Nothing can happen. I am with you.”

After that, Jesus got into the boat with Peter and the other apostles. The wind stopped blowing, and the waters became quiet again.

Another time, the apostles were on the lake fishing. They had worked hard all night.

When morning came, they still had nothing in their nets. How sad they were!

Then they saw Jesus looking at them. He was far away.

Simon Peter cried out, “Lord, we have worked all night, but we have no fish in our nets.”

Jesus called back and said, “Put your nets down on the other side of the boat.”

As soon as the apostles obeyed, their nets were so filled that they were hard to hold.

When they got to the land, Jesus had made a fire to cook the fish. He knew that the apostles were very tired.

After they ate some of the fish from their nets, Our Lord asked, "Do you love Me, Simon Peter?"

And Peter said, "Yes, Lord."

After a little while, Jesus asked Peter the same thing again and again.

"Lord, You know everything," Peter answered. "You know, too, how much I love You."

Our Lord was pleased with Simon Peter. He knew that his love was real. He told Peter that he was to take His place after He went back to His home in heaven. Jesus made Peter the head of His Church.

Peggy and Ginger

Kevin Green was late coming home from school. His little sister Peggy was sitting on the steps waiting for him.

Peggy was four. She loved her big brother and waited for him every afternoon.

"Maybe next year I will go to school," she thought.

She turned to the toy bear at her side. "Maybe you can come to school, too, Ginger," she said in a quiet little voice.

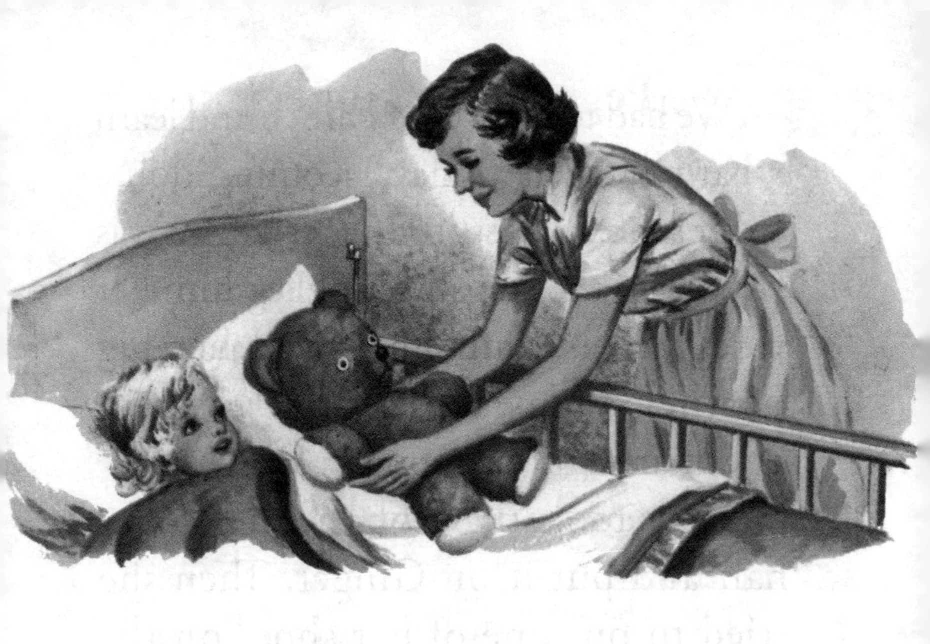

Ginger's one eye almost fell out as Peggy picked him up. He had been her best toy friend for a long time. Uncle Jim had given him to her at her birthday party when she was two.

"He is a beautiful teddy bear," Mother had said when she first saw him. "He is just the color of gingerbread."

So that is how he got his name. Everyone in the family called him Ginger.

"Hello, Kevin!" cried Peggy, as her big brother got off the bus. "You are late!"

"We had to go over to church and learn what to do on Sunday," Kevin said.

Then Kevin went into the house.

"Just think, Ginger," said Peggy to her teddy bear, "Kevin is going to make his First Communion next Sunday. Mother says that Jesus will come to him."

Peggy took the ribbon out of her hair and put it on Ginger. Then she tried to put one of her shoes on the teddy bear's foot.

"First Communion day is even better than a birthday, Ginger," Peggy said. "You get gifts, and Jesus comes to you, too."

Peggy began to feel sad. "What shall we give Kevin for a gift, Ginger? I have no money of my own. Maybe I can draw a picture of you. But I can't draw very well."

"Peggy, please put your shoe on your foot," Mother said. "You don't want to have a cold and go to bed, do you?"

"What are you and Daddy going to give Kevin?" Peggy asked Mother.

Mother smiled. She knew what the little girl was thinking.

"We have a beautiful rosary and prayer book for him," she answered. "We will put your name on the card. Then the gift will be from all three of us."

"But I want to give him something that is from me," said Peggy in a sad way.

"Well, maybe you could do something for your brother," Mother said. "You could make a little altar in his bedroom. I am sure Kevin would like that."

"I guess maybe he would," said Peggy as she walked into the house.

The Sunday after Easter came, and it was time for Kevin's party. Many aunts and uncles came. The table was filled with all kinds of good things to eat.

While Kevin was opening his gifts Peggy left the room. No one missed her.

She walked back into the room with a big box in her arms. It had white paper and blue ribbon around it.

Mother had a strange look on her face. "Oh, dear!" she thought. "What does that child have? And where did she get all the ribbon and paper?"

Daddy smiled. "What is in that box?" he asked Mother.

Kevin began to open the box. He saw something brown. "Why, Peggy, it's your Ginger!" he said.

"Do you like him, Kevin?" Peggy asked. "It was the best gift I could think of."

Kevin didn't know what to say. What could he do with a teddy bear?

Mother looked at Kevin and made a funny face. "What a nice gift!" she said.

Kevin knew what Mother was trying to do. "Oh, it's just the best gift you could give, Peggy. Thank you," he said. "But, you know, I'm at school so much. Do you think you could take care of Ginger for me?"

"Oh, yes!" cried Peggy.

What a happy girl Peggy was! She had given a gift to Kevin that pleased him. And every day she could still play with Ginger.

First Communion Day

At last the happy day of First Holy Communion came for the children of Saint Peter's Parish.

In the Fay home, Karen got up long before the rest of the family. She ran to the window and looked out. The sun was just coming up.

"Oh, what a pretty day!" she said to herself. She said her morning prayer and told Our Lord how happy she was.

Karen was excited and happy as she put on her white shoes and her white dress.

After Karen was dressed, Mother placed a white prayer book and rosary in her hands. "God bless you, dear, on this day," she said.

Then the family walked out to get into the car. One of Karen's little friends saw her. It was Pam White.

"Hello, Karen," called Pam. "How nice you look! Why are you dressed all in white?"

"I am going to church to receive my First Holy Communion," Karen answered.

"I wish I could go along with you," said Pam. "I would like to see you do that."

Pam was not a Catholic. She had never been in a Catholic church.

"May Pam come with us?" Karen asked her father.

"Pam may come along if her parents say it is all right," said Mr. Fay.

"Ask your mother and daddy," Karen said. "Bring your hat, too."

It took only a few minutes for Pam to ask her parents and to get her hat.

On the way to church, Pam asked, "What does it mean to receive your First Holy Communion?"

"It means that I am going to receive Jesus," Karen answered.

"You are?" said Pam in a surprised voice.

"Yes," said Karen. "That is why the boys and girls dress in white. We all want to look nice because Jesus Himself is coming to us in the Sacred Host."

Pam waited at the church door while Mr. and Mrs. Fay went with Karen. They went to the room where the First Communion children were to meet.

James went with the altar boys. Michael went with the boys who were to sing.

Pam opened the door and looked into the church. The altar looked so pretty with the beautiful flowers beside it.

By the time Mr. and Mrs. Fay came back, Pam had many things to ask them.

"Will I see Jesus when He comes to the children?" she asked.

"Yes, but He will not look as He does in pictures," answered Mrs. Fay. "You will see only a round piece of bread which we call the Sacred Host. The Host is only bread until the priest changes it into the Body of Christ in the Mass."

Then Pam went into the church with Mr. and Mrs. Fay. How nice all the boys and girls looked in white!

Pam loved Our Lord. She wished that He would come to her, too.

When the Mass started, the children and all of the grownups prayed with the priest.

At last the happy moment came! It was the Communion of the Mass.

Each child and his parents walked up to the altar. There they waited.

The priest and people all said a prayer together.

Then Father Burns gave the Sacred Host to each one.

At last Jesus had come. The children had received their First Holy Communion. From now on they could receive the Sacred Host every day if they wanted.

A Strange Gift

Carl Cook and his sister Kathy went to Saint Peter's School. At home, they had three brothers and one baby sister.

In the evening, Mrs. Cook would patch the children's clothes. Sometimes she would make wishes.

"Oh, dear," she would say. "I wish I had some different colored thread."

Sometimes she wished for red thread. Sometimes she wished for blue thread.

One afternoon, the children were talking. “Mother’s birthday will be on the same day as the feast of Mary,” Carl said.

“Then we must get two different kinds of gifts ready,” Kathy said. “We need a gift for Mother and a gift for Mary.”

“Let’s pray the Rosary every day,” said Carl, “and offer a crown of roses to Mary.”

“But what kind of gift shall we get for Mother?” Kathy asked.

“Why don’t we get some thread?” Carl said. “We can get a box filled with all different colors. Then Mother will always have the kind of thread she needs.”

“That will be the best gift,” Kathy said. “Let’s save our money for a box of thread.”

Kathy got her little bank that looked like a wishing well.

"Let's put our money in this wishing well," she told Carl and her little brothers.

The children tried hard to save their money. As the days went by, something began to happen in the family.

Carl did not seem to care much about the money in the wishing well. He was always too busy to play. He stayed at school almost every afternoon.

It was all very, very strange.

"What does Carl do at school all the time, Mother?" Kathy asked one day.

"He said that he and Father Denis are working on something," answered Mother.

One evening, Kathy asked her brother if he still wanted to buy the box of thread for Mother's birthday.

"Sure, I do," Carl answered. "But I have another kind of gift to give her, too. It's a gift for both Mother and Mary, our Queen. It's something you can't buy in a store."

The day before Mother's birthday came. Kathy and Daddy went to the dime store to buy the box of colored thread.

The next morning, the children put the box of thread on the table.

When Mother came into the room, they all sang, "Happy Birthday to You!"

Then they all got ready to go to Mass. When it was time to leave the house, no one could find Carl.

"I saw him go out of the door with his prayer book," said one of the boys.

“Then he must have gone to church,” said Mr. Cook.

“But why didn’t he wait and go with us?” asked Mother. “He does on other Sundays. To think he would do a thing like this on Mary’s feast and on my birthday!”

The family tried to be happy, but they could not forget about Carl.

When Father Denis came out to offer Mass, Mother and Daddy were surprised. There was Carl with the priest. He was an altar boy on Mother’s birthday.

How happy and proud Carl's parents were! Now they knew why Carl had stayed after school. They knew, too, why he did not have much time to play.

They both knew why he had gone off to church by himself that morning.

Carl had offered a crown of roses as a feast-day gift for Mary. But this was another gift for both Mary, our Queen in heaven, and for Mother, the queen at home.

It was a gift you cannot buy in a store.

A Great Feast Day

Holy Thursday is one of the great feast days in the Catholic Church. Many people in Saint Peter's Parish go to Mass on that day. They thank Our Lord for the gift of His Body and Blood.

On the first Holy Thursday many years ago Our Lord called two of His apostles.

"Go into the city," He said to them. "Get everything ready so that we can all eat supper there this evening."

"Lord, we do not know anyone in the city," the apostles said. "How shall we find a place in which to have the supper?"

Jesus told the apostles that they would meet a man with a jar filled with water.

"Follow that man to the house where he will go," Jesus said. "There you will meet the owner of the house. Ask the owner for a room for our supper."

The two apostles said good-by to Our Lord and went into the city. There everything happened just as Jesus had said it would.

They met the man with a jar of water. So they followed him and did what Jesus had told them to do.

In the evening, Our Lord and the other ten apostles came to the room where their supper was ready for them.

This was to be Christ's last supper with His apostles. On the next day, He was going to die on the cross for us.

The apostles did not know that. But they could tell that Jesus seemed very sad.

Then they saw Jesus do something He had never done before.

Jesus got a large jar and filled it with water. After that, He began to wash the feet of each apostle.

The apostles did not know what to think. They looked at each other in a strange way.

Jesus knew what the apostles were thinking. But He wanted to show them and us that no one should ever be too proud to help others.

When He had finished washing their feet, He sat down and began to speak to them.

"Be kind to one another," He told them. "I will be with you for only a little while more. Then I must leave you. But before I go, I want to tell you something.

"I shall always know that you love Me if you are kind to others."

The apostles were very surprised and frightened to hear Jesus say that He was going to leave them.

"Where are You going?" Peter asked.

Jesus answered, "Where I am going, you cannot come now. But someday I will come and take you to My home in heaven."

After that, Jesus and the apostles ate the supper that was ready for them.

When the supper was over, everything in the room became very quiet. There was not a sound to be heard.

The apostles looked at Our Lord. He seemed more beautiful than ever before. They saw Him take a piece of bread and bless it.

Then they heard Him say, “Take this and eat, for This is My Body.”

After that Jesus took a cup of wine into His hands. He blessed the wine and said to the apostles, “Take this and drink, for This is My Blood.”

Our Lord had changed bread and wine into His own sacred Body and Blood.

That first Holy Thursday was a great feast day for the apostles and for all of us.

On that day, the apostles received their first Holy Communion. They were made priests, too, because Christ told them to do what He had done. They were to change bread and wine into His Body and Blood.

Now every Catholic priest does what Our Lord did at the Last Supper. He changes bread and wine into the Body and Blood of Christ every time he offers the Mass.

That Sweet Story of Old

I think when I read that sweet story of old,
When Jesus was here among men,
How He called little children as lambs to
  His fold,
I should like to have been with them
  then.
I wish that His hands had been placed on
  my head,
That His arm had been thrown around
  me,
And that I might have seen His kind look
  when He said,
"Let the little ones come unto Me."

Jemima Luke

The Parish Library

Gifts for the Library

One Monday afternoon, Mr. Fay looked at all the books on the table in the living room.

"Well, the Fay family is doing its part for the new library," said Daddy.

"You mean some of the Fay family," said Mother. "Karen has many books, but she does not want to give them to the new library."

The next morning, Mother talked to Karen. "If every child in your school did as you are doing," she said, "we could not have a parish library."

"But, Mother, I am giving up three good storybooks," said Karen in a quiet voice.

Mother picked up the three books. The first one was very old. The second had red paint on it. And the other one was not even clean.

"Why have you picked out these three books?" Mother asked Karen.

"Well, I don't want them any more," answered Karen.

"Do you think other children will want to use them?" asked Mother.

"You don't want me to give away my good books, do you?" asked Karen.

"You don't have to give them," Mother said. "But it would be nice to let other children use your books.

"Of course, you would be helping the parish, too. The new library is for all the people in the parish."

Karen sat still for a few moments. Then she looked at her books again.

Just then Michael called, "We will be late for school if you don't hurry, Karen."

So Karen started off to school with her two brothers.

Michael and James both had their arms full of books for the new parish library.

"I'll help you carry some of those," Karen offered.

"Where are your books for the library? Didn't you pick some out?" asked James.

"I had three to give, but Mother said they are not good enough," answered Karen.

The Fay children saw many other boys and girls with their arms full of books.

Karen was the only one who did not have a book for the library. She began to feel strange and tried to keep quiet.

All at once she saw Ann with only one book under her arm.

"One book is not very much," Karen thought. She ran to catch up with Ann.

She looked at the book that Ann had. It had very pretty drawings in it, and it looked almost new.

"Are you going to give that nice book to the parish library?" Karen asked.

"Yes, it is the only good book I own," her friend answered. "I received it for my birthday a few weeks ago."

"Why don't you keep it?" asked Karen.

"My mother told me it would be nice to let other children use it," Ann said.

All morning, Karen thought about Ann's book with the pretty drawings.

At lunch time, Karen told her mother about the storybook Ann had given away.

You can guess what Karen did with her books after that. Yes, she gave most of them to the library.

The Apron Calendar

There were all kinds of books in the new parish library. Books about trees, animals, birds, funny stories, and holy books about God and the saints.

Here are some of the stories the children read in their new library.

One day, Grandmother Turner lost her one and only calendar.

"Oh, dear me!" she cried. "Now how shall I know what day of the week it is?"

Grandmother sat down in her chair. She thought and thought.

"I know what I can do," said Grandmother. "I shall make an apron calendar. I will use a different color for each day."

So Grandmother got her thread and other things. She made a blue apron for Monday.

"I shall wear this one on wash day," she said to herself.

The second apron she made was a red one for Tuesday. That was the day on which she patched clothes.

"I must have something pretty to wear to my club meeting on Wednesday afternoon," thought Grandmother. So she picked yellow for Wednesday.

Grandmother always worked and planted things in her garden on Thursday. So she picked green for that day and made a green apron.

On Friday, Grandmother always went to town to buy food for the week. She made a pink apron to wear on Fridays.

She made a brown apron to wear on Saturdays when she cleaned the house and made bread. For Sundays, she made a pretty white apron to wear to church.

Then all seven aprons were finished. Grandmother put them into a box just the way they should have been.

The box was full of aprons. Blue for Monday. Red for Tuesday. Yellow for Wednesday. Green for Thursday. Pink for Friday. Brown for Saturday. And white for Sunday.

Then Grandmother was tired so she went to bed. While she was sleeping, her dog Cracker pulled the box of aprons off the chair. When the aprons fell, they got all mixed up.

In the morning, Grandmother did not know what to do. "I am sure this must be Friday," she said to herself. So she put on her pink apron and went to town.

She missed her friend, Mrs. Jay, who was always downtown on the same day.

The next day, Grandmother put on her brown apron and cleaned the house. She was surprised to see school children going up the street, but she went right on working.

The next morning, Grandmother put on her pretty white apron and went to church. How surprised she was! The church was dark and quiet.

"Well, it seems that everyone is going to be late today," she thought.

It was so quiet Grandmother went to sleep. When she opened her eyes, the church was still dark, and she was alone.

"Oh, me!" she said. "I must have been sleeping while prayers were going on."

The next day was wash day. That is what Grandmother thought! She put on her blue apron and washed her clothes.

People were all dressed up as they walked by the house. Almost everyone stopped to look at Grandmother washing her clothes.

But Grandmother thought nothing of it. She went right on with her work.

When she got up the next day, she put on her red apron and did Tuesday's work.

Grandmother was wearing the yellow apron when she went to the club meeting the next day. No one was there. She waited and waited, but no one came.

On the way home, Grandmother met Mrs. Long. "Why didn't you come to the club meeting this afternoon?" Grandmother asked her.

"We don't meet until tomorrow. This is only Tuesday," laughed Mrs. Long. "You must have your days mixed up."

Grandmother ran home. She got out the apron box.

"One, two, three, four, five, six," she said. "Why, there are only six aprons here! There should be seven."

She looked all over the house for the missing apron. At last she found the green one under the bed.

"That's it!" she laughed. "I had my days all mixed up. I went to church on Saturday and washed clothes on Sunday! I do need a real calendar."

And the very next day, Grandmother got a new calendar.

A Letter to Heaven

One day, when Joseph was small, his mother sent him to get some bread.

"May I get a bottle of milk, too?" Joseph asked his mother.

"No, Joseph, there is not enough money for milk," his mother said in a sad way.

As he walked to the store, Joseph began to think of the many things his family could not have. They did not have much money.

But Joseph did not know how poor his parents really were until he heard them talking that night.

"Our new baby will be coming soon," said Joseph's mother. "How shall we ever buy food and clothes for it?"

"I will try to find more work to do," answered Joseph's father. "We will get along somehow. We always do."

Joseph began to feel strange and unhappy. The very next day, he told the pastor of his parish what he had heard.

"Joseph," said the kind old priest, "you must pray to Our Father in heaven. He is giving the new baby to your family. He will see that the little one is cared for."

Joseph began to go to church every day after that and pray to Our Father.

One Monday afternoon, Joseph thought of something to do.

He had one toy that he liked very, very much. It was a red balloon that his father had given him.

That afternoon, he took the red balloon and a small piece of paper. He ran to a place near his father's barn.

Then he began to write words on the piece of paper. He put the paper on the balloon and sent it up into the sky.

Away went the red balloon carrying Joseph's paper.

Two weeks went by. Then one day the mailman left a large box at Joseph's house. It had come from another town.

"This cannot be for us," Joseph's mother told the mailman. "We don't even know anyone in that town."

"But look, it has your name on it," said the mailman. "The name of the street is right, too."

So Joseph's mother opened the box. What a surprise she had!

There on top was a little piece of paper for Joseph. It said, "Dear Joseph, this is for your new baby brother."

Under the paper, Mother found beautiful baby clothes.

The next week another box came. Then almost every day more boxes were sent.

There were toys, baby food, warm clothes, and even money for the new baby.

Joseph's parents and the parish priest did not know what to think. Over and over again they asked Joseph what he had said on the piece of paper that went up with the red balloon.

"Dear God," he had said, "I am going to have a little baby brother. Mother and Daddy are poor. Please give us the things we need for my little brother."

Joseph also told the name of the street and the town in which he lived.

Some people thought the red balloon had landed in another town. There, some kind people had read Joseph's letter. Then they sent the surprises to his home.

But Joseph always said that his red balloon went right up to God. And God told those kind people to help his family.

The Saint Who Did Tricks

Little John Bosco lived in this world many years ago. He liked all the things other boys like—candy, cake, ice cream, and all kinds of good food.

John was a very good ball player. All the neighbor boys liked to play with him.

After John was ten years old, he began to dream about being a priest someday. So he went to Mass every day, and he worked hard at school.

John knew that if he really wanted to be a priest, it would take many years of work.

One day, John's father took him to a fair. There he saw a man doing all kinds of funny tricks.

John liked the tricks very much. He looked to see how the man did them.

That evening, when John got home, he tried some of the tricks.

From that day on, John used those tricks in his work for God. This is how he did it.

Not far from John's home there were many boys who were not very good. They stayed away from Mass on Sundays.

They did not pray very much. Many of these poor boys really did not know much about the good God.

One Tuesday afternoon, John Bosco asked all the boys to come to his father's barn. When they got there, he did some of his funny tricks for them.

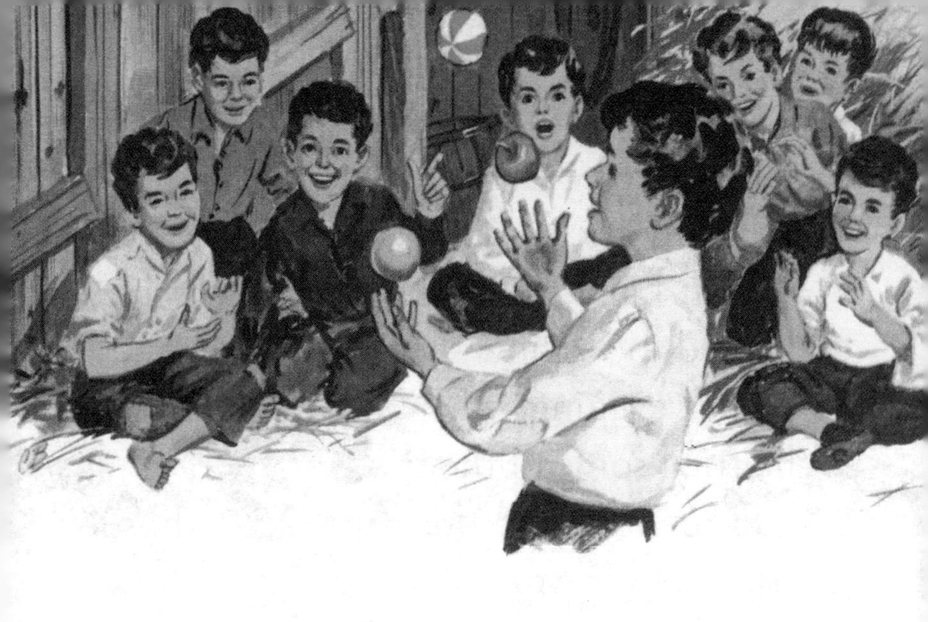

"More, John! Give us some more!" the boys called every time John stopped his tricks.

"All right," answered John, "but first let's all pray the Rosary together." Then the boys prayed the Rosary.

Soon John Bosco became a teacher for all the boys in town. He taught them many kinds of games. But, at the same time, he taught them about God.

When John was older, he said good-by to his family. He went to become a priest.

One morning when Father John Bosco walked into the church to offer Mass, he found a poor little boy waiting for him.

"What can I do for you?" the kind priest asked the boy.

"Oh, Father," said the boy. "I just came in here to get warm. It is so cold outside. I have no home. Both of my parents died two years ago."

"Stay right here and get warm," Father John told the little boy. "I need a boy like you to help me."

Then the priest asked, "Do you know any prayers, my boy?"

"No, I have never learned any," answered the boy.

Father John began right away to teach the boy how to pray the Our Father.

"Father John," the boy said. "If I bring my friends here next week, will you teach all of us some more things?"

"I'll be glad to," smiled the kind priest. "You may bring as many of your friends as you like."

So the next Sunday, the little boy came with eight other boys. And every Sunday after that more and more boys came. They wanted to hear Father John Bosco talk about the good God.

Soon there were many boys. So the priest had to find a larger place for them to meet.

Many of these boys had no homes. So Father John Bosco worked and worked until he could buy a big old house. Then he and his boys went there to live together.

All the boys helped to clean the house and fix it up. They even made the tables, chairs, beds, and other things.

Then Father John taught the boys to read and write and draw beautiful pictures.

He even taught them to fix shoes, make clothes, make bread from wheat, and do different kinds of work so they could make some money.

After a few years, some of the older boys in Father John Bosco's school wanted to become priests.

Now Father John Bosco is a saint in heaven. There are many priests all over the world doing the work he started many years ago.

The Hat with Cherries on It

Patty stood before the looking glass. She turned this way and that way. How pretty her pink dress looked!

"Hold still, dear!" said her mother. "I want to put your new hat on."

The hat was a pretty white one with cherries on it. The cherries looked real and almost good enough to eat.

"Here is Joan's birthday gift," said Mother. "Now, be a good girl and have a nice time. Look at the lights when you cross Second Street."

It was a nice warm day. Patty went to the party and had a good time.

On the way home, the wind began to blow. It blew Patty's new white hat right off her head.

The wind began to carry the hat out into the street. Patty did not even try to run after it. There were too many cars and trucks in the street for her to do that.

She waited for the lights to change. Then she looked as far as she could see. But the hat with cherries on it was nowhere to be seen.

Patty asked some of the people on the sidewalk if they had seen her hat.

Patty even asked a newsboy sitting on the steps of a house. But no one had seen the pretty white hat with cherries on it.

Patty was crying when she got home.

"Don't cry, dear," said her mother. We will buy another hat."

Patty's mother did buy her another new hat, but it did not have cherries on it.

Weeks went by, and Patty began to forget about the white hat with cherries on it.

Then one warm day, Patty was out in the yard playing with her dolls. She heard a strange sound out on the street.

When she looked up, she saw an old wagon filled with paper, rags, and trash of all kinds. The wagon was pulled by an old tired-looking horse.

Patty looked hard at the horse. For a moment she thought she was seeing things.

The horse was wearing a hat with red cherries on it. There were two big holes in it for the horse's ears.

Patty knew at once that it was her hat. She ran to the street and waved to the man in the wagon.

"Any paper, rags, or trash today?" he asked as he stopped his horse.

"Oh, no," answered Patty. "But where did you get that hat?"

"You know, that hat came right down from heaven," the man said. "Yes, it did. It came right down out of the sky."

"But where did you get it?" Patty asked.

"Well," said the man, "I was near Second Street one Wednesday.

"My horse was feeling bad. For a while, I thought she was going to die. She just could not take the hot sun.

"Then all at once, out of the blue sky, came this white hat with cherries on it. My horse liked it the minute she saw it. I fixed it up and put it on her head. And now she is like a new horse."

"That is my hat," said Patty. "It blew off my head that day."

"Well, what do you know!" said the man with a sad look on his face. "You don't want it back, do you, little lady?"

"No, I guess not," Patty answered. "If it has made your horse so happy, you had better keep it."

The old horse looked very happy as she pulled the wagon on down the street.

The King of the Fishes

Once upon a time, there lived a little farm girl named Candy. Her job was to take care of the geese.

One warm day, Candy took the geese down to the pond to get a drink.

While the geese were drinking, Candy put her hands into the water and pulled out a large gold fish.

To her surprise, the fish began to speak to her. This is what it said:

"Little girl, little girl,
Please let me free,
Or ever after this
Sorry you will be."

“Oh, my!” cried Candy. You must be a magic fish!”

“Let me go free!” cried the fish. “No!” said Candy.

“Please, let me go free,” said the fish. “No,” said Candy again.

Then the fish tried something different. He said,

> “Let me go free!
> Let me go free!
> I’m the king of the fishes.
> And if you let me go,
> I’ll give you three wishes.”

“All right,” said Candy. “I wish to be a princess and have all kinds of maids to wait on me.”

“Wait! Wait!” cried the fish. “Don’t make any more wishes now. You just used your first and second wishes. Save the last wish for a while.”

"Then how will I find you?" asked Candy. "I'll be here," said the fish. "All you have to do is to call me and say,

'Come to me! Come to me,
King of the fishes!
I'm ready to ask
For the last of my wishes.'"

Then the fish went into the water. Candy looked at herself in the water. On her head was a crown of gold. Her dress, too, had been changed into gold.

Her geese had all been changed into maids, and they began to follow her home.

Candy's mother was waiting at the door for her. She looked different. She had a crown on her head and was dressed like a queen, but she looked very unhappy.

"Candy, what has happened to us?" cried the mother. "I was busy making an apple pie when all at once everything changed. My apron changed into this long dress. My white cap became a gold crown."

Candy told her mother what had happened at the pond. But her mother was not pleased. She liked to do her own cooking and cleaning. Now, as a queen, she had nothing to do.

For about ten weeks, Candy was pleased with her new way of living. But after that, she became unhappy.

Her friends no longer played with her. They were children of working people. They could not play with a princess.

Then one day Candy saw Bill coming.

"Oh, Bill!" she cried. "At last you are coming to see me!"

"No, I am not," answered Bill. "I have come only to bring some milk to your cook. A poor boy like me cannot play with a princess."

After a few days, Candy began to see how silly her new way of living was. So she ran down to the pond and cried,

> "Come to me! Come to me,
> King of the fishes!
> I'm ready to ask
> For the last of my wishes."

The gold fish came up at once. He began to speak, "I'm sure I know what your last wish is," he said. "You don't want to be a princess any longer, do you?"

"That's it!" cried Candy in an excited way. "Please change me back into a poor little girl just as fast as you can."

So at once Candy became a poor little farm girl again. The maids were changed back into geese.

Best of all, Bill and Candy's other little friends all came to play with her again.

The Laughingest Family

"Six bells and all is well!" cried a man as he went up the street.

At the sound of his voice, the little Peggy children opened their eyes.

"All is well!" they cried as they clapped their hands.

"The sun is so bright," said the oldest one.

"The birds are singing!" said the in-between-one.

"The princess is coming to town today!" cried the smallest one, "the princess who never laughs!"

Just then Wee-Wee-Old-Grandmother looked into the room. "Jumping turtles! What's all the talking about?" she asked.

"The princess is coming today," cried the in-between-one.

"We will be sure to make her laugh," said the oldest one.

"We are the laughingest family in the town," said the smallest one.

Wee-Wee-Old-Grandmother shook her head. "I'm not so sure about that," she said. "There are times, you know."

"But today we will laugh for sure," said the in-between-one. "Just think, there is a princess who never laughs!"

After breakfast, the three little Peggys put on their very best clothes. Then they sat down to wait for their Uncle Pete.

He was going to take them to the town hall. That's where the princess would be.

They waited and they laughed and they waited.

At nine o'clock, a man came up the hill to the house.

"Your Uncle Pete can't come this morning," said the man. "He is helping his neighbors to clean out their chimney." Then the little Peggys were very sad.

You would never think that so much crying could come from the laughingest family. But it did.

"That's just like Uncle Pete," cried the oldest one.

"Why can't he clean their chimney tomorrow?" cried the in-between-one.

"Now we can't make the princess laugh," cried the smallest one.

Then they cried louder and louder.

At that very moment, Grandmother said, "Jumping turtles! You laugh only when things go your way. You must learn to laugh when things go wrong, too. If not, you will never make others laugh."

The three little Peggys changed their good clothes and put on their older ones.

Then they got busy at once and began to help clean the house. They began to laugh as they worked.

At ten o'clock, they were laughing and making the bed when they heard someone at the door.

Grandmother opened the door. There stood a tall man with a little girl.

"I heard someone laughing so I thought we should stop in," said the man.

"Come right in," said Grandmother. "There is always someone laughing in this house. We are called the laughingest family in town."

The little girl went into the room where the Peggy children were working.

"I was on my way to the town hall," the man told Grandmother. Then he stopped.

"What, what, what is that?" he asked.

"That is the best sound in all the world," said Wee-Wee-Old-Grandmother. "It is the sound of children laughing."

"But they are all laughing—my own child, too!" said the surprised man, as he looked into the room where the children were.

"Of course," answered Grandmother.

"This has been a great day for me," said the tall man. "Now I can go back home without going to the town hall."

As the man started out of the house he said, "Come, my princess!"

The Peggy children looked at each other in surprise.

"That was the princess!" said the oldest one.

"And we made her laugh!" said the in-between-one.

"And she will keep on laughing every day!" said the smallest one.

Wee-Wee-Old-Grandmother looked at the three children. "You had a right to make her laugh," she said. "Today you learned to laugh even when things went wrong."

"Now we really are the laughingest family in town," said the smallest one.

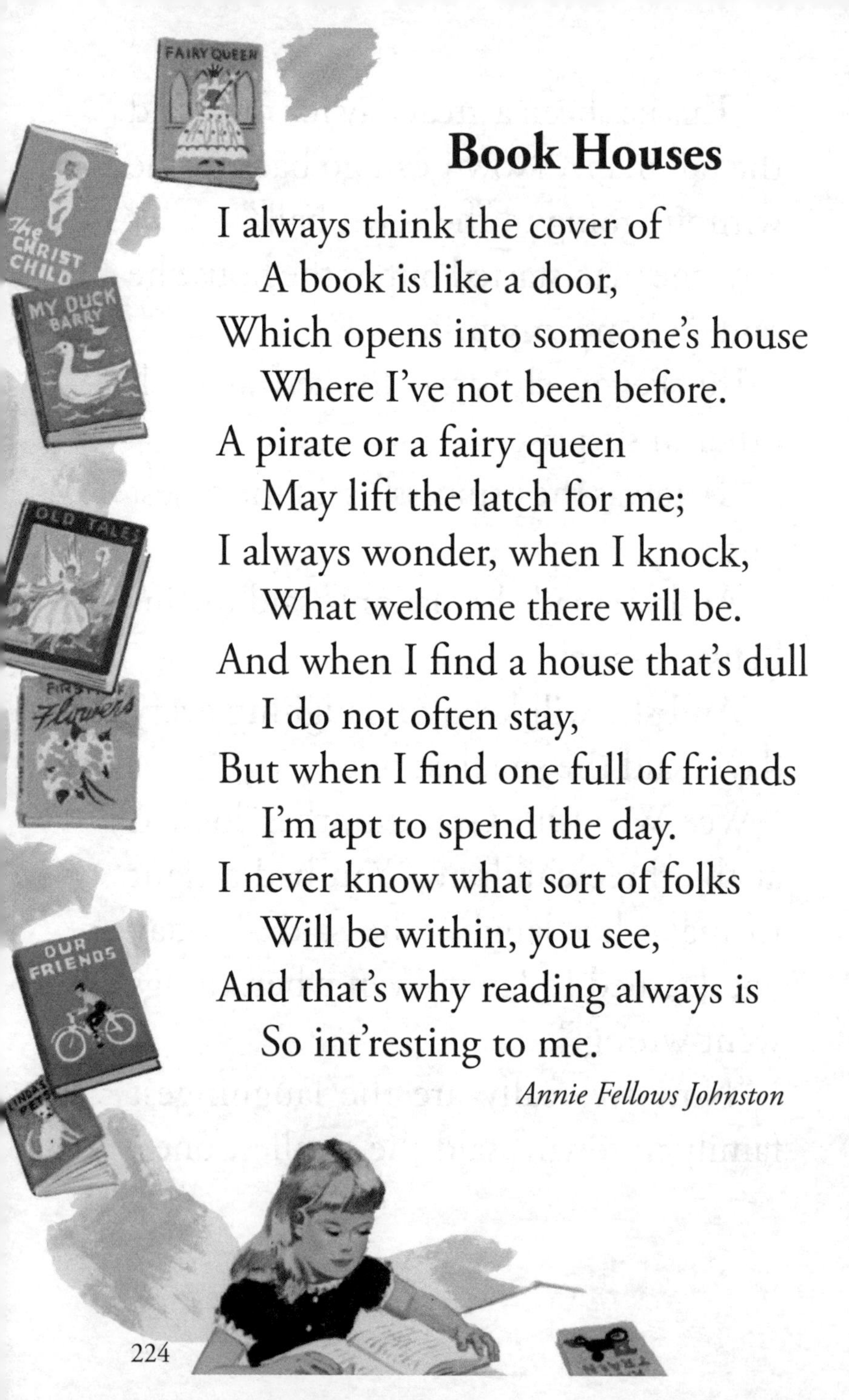

Book Houses

I always think the cover of
  A book is like a door,
Which opens into someone's house
  Where I've not been before.
A pirate or a fairy queen
  May lift the latch for me;
I always wonder, when I knock,
  What welcome there will be.
And when I find a house that's dull
  I do not often stay,
But when I find one full of friends
  I'm apt to spend the day.
I never know what sort of folks
  Will be within, you see,
And that's why reading always is
  So int'resting to me.

Annie Fellows Johnston

Good Times Together

The Merry Magic Show

The Cubs of Saint Peter's Parish wanted to have a show.

"What kind of show can we have?" asked Mr. Hall, their helper.

"I know," said Freddy Brown. "We can have a cowboy show."

"What about a magic show?" said another boy. "We can do some of the tricks we have learned."

"We could have an animal show, too," said Tim Waters.

"If we put all three kinds of shows together," said Mr. Hall, "maybe we will have one good big one. How will that be?"

"Fine!" cried the Cubs. "We will call it The Merry Magic Show."

For eight weeks, the boys were busy getting ready for the show. Every Monday and Wednesday evening, Mr. Hall helped them.

"It must be really good if we want people to buy tickets for it," he told the boys.

The Cubs were going to use the money from the show to pay for a trip.

They wanted to go to Rock City. There they would see some of the new jet planes. So they worked to make their show good.

Michael had to learn how to change a green balloon into something that looked like a frog. Every time he did it, he laughed and laughed.

"You must not laugh in the show," Mr. Hall told Michael. "If you do, you will give the trick away, and your frog will not look real."

Ted was a small boy. In the show he was to be dressed up like a big green worm. When James held up a wand, the worm changed into a butterfly.

Pete learned to throw three balls at one time. He had to keep them from falling.

"Maybe I'll be like Saint John Bosco," he told the boys as he did his trick.

"I wish we knew some of the tricks Saint John Bosco taught," said Mr. Hall.

At last the night for the real show came. Every Cub Scout had a job. Some of them were selling tickets at the door. Some took tickets from people as they came into the hall.

Some of the boys helped people find places to sit. They gave the pastor and Father Denis the best places.

After a little while, the lights went out and the show began.

Tim Waters came out and said, "The Cub Scouts of Saint Peter's Parish have become the world's best magic makers. Tonight you will see and hear things you have never seen or heard before."

Bang! Bang! Bang!

Tim jumped. He looked frightened. "What in the world is that?" he thought. "That was not part of our show."

Bang! Bang! Bang!

This time Tim was so excited that he cried, "What is that?"

The people laughed and laughed. They thought what they heard was part of The Merry Magic Show. But it was not.

Again everyone heard the strange sound. Bang! Bang! Bow-wow! Bow-wow! Bang!

"A dog!" cried Michael.

The boys looked. The sounds were coming from under the table.

"My dog!" said Freddy in a voice that did not sound very happy. "Look what he has done!"

Freddy's dog had jumped into the box of balloons that was under the table. Every balloon was broken.

"Well, that was one trick which we did not think of using," said Mr. Hall. "Come on, boys, the show must go on."

Mr. Hall told the people what had happened. The people laughed more than ever. They clapped and clapped when Freddy showed them the dog that had stopped the show.

Some of the tricks for which balloons were needed could not be done. But the rest of the show was good.

Michael had not put his balloon under the table. It was in a different place.

So he changed it into a thing that looked like a frog. And all the Cub Scouts sang this song:

"Oh, see the big green ball,
The big green ball,
The big green ball.
Oh, see the big green ball.
But look! It's not a ball at all."

Then the people clapped and clapped. They thought it was a fine show.

The Parish Fair

Every year, the people of Saint Peter's Parish had a fair.

The money made at the fair was used to help poor boys who wanted to be priests.

Everyone worked hard to make the fair a good one. The mothers made all kinds of pretty things. The fathers fixed up little places that looked like stores.

The children gave small toys and other things to be used in the fish pond.

At last, everything was finished. So Father Burns told the people that the fair would open on Friday evening.

That afternoon, Mark Stone asked Father Burns something. "May we please see how the fair looks before we go home?"

"Yes, each room may go to the hall to see the fair," said the pastor.

"Tomorrow is Saturday," he said. "So tomorrow afternoon you may all come and have a good time at the fair."

"I want to fish for a surprise," said Michael.

"So do I," said another boy. "That is always the best part of a fair."

The boys and girls were excited when they saw all the nice things at the fair.

There were pretty colored ribbons, bright pins, cups, toy roosters, vases, aprons, warm baby caps and shoes, footballs, and many other things.

There was one store called Toyland. All the small children liked that store the best. In it there were funny pigs, toy mules, a calf, a funny goose, toy soldiers, balloons, toy dishes and cups, toy telephones, baby dolls, and doll clothes.

As the children walked around, Father Denis heard one of them say something. It was a boy named Martin.

"I wish I could come to the fair tomorrow," he told his friends. "My daddy has been out of work for a long time. So Mother says we must save every cent."

Father Denis called Martin. As he talked to him, he put fifty cents into the boy's pocket. "Come and have a good time tomorrow," said the priest.

Martin thanked Father. He said, "Maybe I will win something nice to take home to my little brother and sister."

The boys and girls had a good time at the fair on Saturday afternoon, too.

Martin saved his money until he saw a pretty paper cup full of candy. "I wish I could win that for my little brother and sister," he said.

Martin tried, but he did not win the cup of candy.

Then he went to the fish pond to try to win something. He pulled out a card. On it were these words: "You are the winner of a basket of food. Go to the table and get it."

Martin could not keep still. He was so happy when he saw how full the basket was. In it were eggs, cans of beans, carrots, apples, and some butter.

The basket was too large for Martin to carry home. So Father Denis offered to help him. "We can go in the car," he said.

Martin was proud and happy as he rode home with the priest.

When they reached Martin's home, he thanked Father Denis for all he had done.

"This has really been the best fair of all," he said.

A Parish Club

Saint Peter's Players was a parish club. Grownups and children were in the club. Every year the players had three big shows. Here is one of the shows they had.

Part I

TIME. Ten o'clock in the morning

PLACE. A flower garden near the woods

READER 1. Once upon a time there was a fairy named Bossy Betty who liked everyone to do just what she wanted.

Her wand helped her to do this. So she always had her wand with her. One day she was in the garden looking for someone to help her.

BOSSY BETTY. Someone must take me to see the Fairy King from Ring-Ting.

WILLY WORM (*looking up from his place in the ground*). Hello, Bossy Betty!

BOSSY BETTY (*jumps*). Keep quiet, you silly worm. Don't talk so loud. Your loud voice will frighten everyone away. And I want someone to carry me to see the Fairy King of Ring-Ting. So be quiet or I'll change you into a rose bug.

WILLY WORM (*backing into the ground*). I guess no one but a worm wants to be a worm. But I don't want to be a rose bug.

BUSY BEE (*flying around some roses*). Why, hello, Bossy Betty.

BOSSY BETTY. Don't talk so loud, Busy Bee. Take me to see the Fairy King from Ring-Ting.

BUSY BEE. I'm too busy.

BOSSY BETTY. Take me or I'll change you into a pumpkin seed.

BUSY BEE (*making a face*). Oh, pancakes! Hop on my back.

READER 1. So away flew Busy Bee. He flew so fast that he almost went by the butternut tree. That is where the Fairy King would be.

Part II

TIME. In the afternoon

PLACE. Under the butternut tree

READER 2. After Bossy Betty had seen the Fairy King of Ring-Ting, it began to rain. She looked around. Up in a tree she saw a very small wing.

BOSSY BETTY (*looking up into the tree*). Why, it's Milly Butterfly. Milly, come down here at once and carry me home.

MILLY BUTTERFLY (*frightened*). I can't take you home in all this rain.

BOSSY BETTY. Take me home at once, or I'll change you into a firefly.

MILLY BUTTERFLY. Oh, all right.

READER 2. It was hard for Milly to fly in the rain. So she stopped to rest on top of a large flower. All at once, Flossy Cow came along to look for something to eat just where Milly was resting.

BOSSY BETTY. Stop that, Flossy Cow.

FLOSSY COW. Oh, I'm sorry. I was so hungry that I just didn't see you.

BOSSY BETTY. Well, you see us now. Go away. We are resting.

READER 2. The cow was trying to turn around when she moved the flower. Milly went flying up and away, and the fairy fell into the brook. Now the fairy was very, very cross at Flossy Cow.

BOSSY BETTY (*cross voice*). Just look at what you have done to me, Flossy Cow. My pink dress has water all over it.

FREDDY FROG (*smiling as he comes up beside Bossy Betty*). Don't talk so loud.

BOSSY BETTY. Freddy Frog, what makes you smile like that?

FREDDY FROG (*smiling more*). I guess I just smile all the time.

BOSSY BETTY. Well, stop smiling, or I'll change you into a— (*Her wand falls into the water.*) Oh, my wand fell. Find it, Freddy. I want it this very moment.

FREDDY FROG. That will not be hard to do. (Finds the wand, but does not pick it up.)

BOSSY BETTY. Wee! I'm glad you found it. Now, get it for me, at once.

FREDDY FROG (*proud voice*). My friend, I'm in no hurry to help you. You can't do anything without your wand. Now you can't change me into a horsefly or a worm. (Frog begins to hop away.)

BOSSY BETTY (*begins to run after the frog*). Stop! Don't go away.

FREDDY FROG. Good-by. I'm on my way to the Tree Frog's Dinner.

BOSSY BETTY (*sad voice*). Oh, Freddy. Please come back and get my wand.

FREDDY FROG (smiling). When you say "please," I will do anything.

BOSSY BETTY (*taking wand from Freddy Frog*). Thank you, Freddy. I can do nothing without my wand. Now I wish I could do something nice for you.

FREDDY FROG. Could you change these weeds into bug butter for me?

BOSSY BETTY (*holding her wand over the weeds*). Of course.

FREDDY FROG (looking at the bug butter). That wand is a pretty handy thing.

BOSSY BETTY (*sad voice*). Yes, it is. But it can't carry me home.

FREDDY FROG. How did you get this far?

BOSSY BETTY. Milly Butterfly helped me. But she flew away and left me here.

FREDDY FROG. Your friends are not very kind to you.

BOSSY BETTY. But I am not kind. From now on I'm going to be different.

FREDDY FROG (begins to smile more). NO one likes to help a bossy fairy. We all like others to be kind to us. There's Blue Jay. I'm sure he will take you home.

READER 2. Blue Jay took the fairy to her home near the garden. Betty tried hard and she was never bossy again. And she always remembered Freddy Frog. Every time she went by the pond she changed the patch of weeds into bug butter or something good for him to eat.

The Parish Party

Besides a fair each year, Saint Peter's Parish also had a big supper party.

If the day was nice, it was a garden party. If it rained or was too cold, the party would be in the parish hall.

The warm days were here again. So it was time to get ready for the parish party.

All the families in the parish helped. School children, their older brothers and sisters, fathers and mothers, and even grandfathers and grandmothers all helped in some way.

Each mother gave the kind of food her family liked best.

When the day for the party came, the sun was out and it was warm. So the supper could be outdoors.

All the children helped to carry baskets and tall boxes of food into the schoolyard.

They knew there would be all the chicken a hungry boy or girl could eat. There would be homemade bread, pies, ginger cookies, and buns.

There would be cream cake filled with nuts. There would be pretty little cakes with pretty colors on top of them.

At six o'clock in the evening Father Burns stood at the gate to meet the people as they came to the party. School boys and girls stood near by to help the grownups to their places.

It was time to begin the supper. The people were given dishes and cups. They took them to the long tables where they took different kinds of good food.

When all the tables were filled, all the people prayed together and thanked God for their food. Then the school band began to play.

After the people were finished eating, Father Burns said, "Let's sing some of the songs we all know. Let's begin with our own country's song."

All the people stood up and sang the song they knew so well.

After that they sang many other different kinds of songs. The last one they sang was "Holy God."

By that time it was dark, and many of the people began to say good-by to one another.

The pastor looked at his big family as they left the party. He loved them all. Boys and girls, fathers and mothers, grandfathers and grandmothers, all were his children.

They worked well together. They had their good times together. They prayed together. And they were so good about helping each other, their neighbors, and their country.

Father Burns was glad that he was their pastor. He was glad that God had picked him to offer Holy Mass for them.

The pastor looked over at the church.

It was getting dark. But Father Burns could see the little light burning in the church.

"Thank You, dear Lord," he prayed. "Thank you for letting me teach this big family to know You and love You. Thank You for letting me help them on their way to heaven.

"Please help me, dear Lord, to be a good, kind father to each and every one of them. Bless them all and keep them always near You."

God's House

God's house is wide and very tall,
The mountains serve Him for a wall;
The roof is arched and blue and high,
And starry-studded—it's the sky!
God's house is beautiful with light,
By day and night He keeps it bright;
He loves His house; He built it all—
The sky, the sea, the mountain-wall.
God's house is open wide, and free,
He lets us live here, you and me,
And we who love His house may tell
Of God's house that He built so well.

Annette Wynne

To the Teacher

This Is Our Parish, Revised Edition, is the Advanced Second Reader of the FAITH AND FREEDOM Basic Readers and is to be used after the completion of *These Are Our Neighbors,* Revised Edition. This reader introduces 240 new basic words, 203 of which (starred in the list below) can be recognized independently through the application of the various word-recognition techniques developed in the teaching manuals of the series and reviewed in the manual accompanying this present text.

Further growth in Christian social living is provided for through story material based on the Catholic child's experiences in the life of the parish, church, and school. The book aims to develop a deeper understanding and appreciation of parochial relationships, a realization of the need for active and cooperative participation in the spiritual and material functions of the parish, and a lasting interest in parish life and activities.

WORD LIST

UNIT I

7. parish

---

8. Fairlands* Fay* town*
9. James* Michael Karen
10. Catholic*
11. means*
12. teach*

---

13. spooky*
14. nine* wall*
15. bump* sound*
16. answered
17. chimney* scampered*
18. meeting* jacket*
19. . . .
20. hold* pastor
21. . . .
22. . . .
23. Cub* Scouts*

---

24. zipper* triplets* arm*
25. until* yard*
26. pulled
27. . . .
28. seven*
29. become*
30. gifts* offer*
31. wine* body*
32. supper* blood•
33. . . .
34. holy* bell*
35. moment* Christ

---

36. throw*
37. hear* window*
38. broke*
39. didn't*
40. late* stood*
41. sorry
42. . . .
43. glad* Blessed*

---

44. umbrella* Mandy* Muggins*
45. . . .
46. . . .
47. . . .
48. course
49. turtle*

---

50. yet* families*
51. . . .
52. afternoon*
53. . . .
54. chicken*

55. Saturday*

---

56. *(Poem)*

UNIT II

57. learning

---

58. wedding*
feast*
59, almost
gone
60. six*
jars*
fill*
61. head*
changed*

---

62. country
parents*
63. Communion
buy*
64. statue*
child
65. voice
babies*
66. nice*
67. grew*
songs*

---

68. brownies*
wife*
69. step*
70. elf*
maids*
71. danced*
oak*
72. sitting*
dream*
73. pond*
twist*
74. different
75. might*

---

76. eight
77. left*
signs
78. quiet*
colors*
79. done
80. . . .

---

81. club*
mission
82. fine*
83. . . .
84. mission-
aries
sell*
85. stamps*
bank*
86. bottle*
doll*

---

87. Easter*
baskets*
88. eyes
bright*
89. falling*
hospital*
90. . . .
91. wrong*
92. sure
those*
93. sent*

---

94. *(Poem)*

UNIT III

95. . . .

---

96. tricks*
most*

---

97. Maria
speak*
98.
99. music
clap*
100. ready*
feet*
101. . . .

---

102. Lippity-
Lop
Company
Chipmunk*
103. trash*
104. finished*
105. through
minutes*
106. leaves*
107. . . .
108. . . .
109. I'll*

---

110. bear*
hot*
111. drink*
smallest*
112. oldest*
noses'
113. worm*
tee-hee*
114. tickled*
115. swim*

---

116. circus
Jingo*
117. follow*
clowns*
118. remember
119. fished*
120. alone*
hard*

---

121. Van Jan*
Carl*
122. tiny*
tall*
123. stones*
124. enough
125. unhappy*
126. fifty'

---

127. Corky*
rooster'
128. Rags*
129. Bossy*
130. . . .
131. skates*
carry
132. foot*
face*
133. proud*

---

134. palace*
upon*
135. also*
I'm*
136. . . .
137. ribbon*
138. . . .
139. bath*

---

140. (*Poem*)

UNIT IV

141. . . .

---

142. . . .
143. vases*
144. large*
excited*
145. fell*
146. Gates*
cents*
147. . . .

---

148. year*
along*
149. apostles
Simon*
150. while*
nothing
151. . . .
152. still*
nets*
153. . . .

---

154. Peggy*
Ginger*
155. . . .
156. draw*
157. . . .
158. table*
159. . . .
160. . . .

---

161. . . .

162. receive*
163. few*
164. Sacred* Host*
165. piece
166. . . .

---

167. thread*
168. crown* roses*
169. . . .
170. both* queen*
171. . . .
172. . . .

---

173. Thursday*
174. . . .
175. ten*
176. . . .
177. . . .
178. cup*
179. . . .

---

180. (*Poem*)

UNIT V

181. . . .

---

182. Monday*
183. second
184. full*
185. under*
186. . . .

---

187. calendar*
188. Tuesday* Wednesday*
189. Friday* pink*
190. . . .
191. . . .
192. . . .
193. . . .

---

194. really*
195. . . .
196. balloon
197. . . .
198. . . .

---

199. John* Bosco*
200. . . .
201. . . .
202. . . .
203. . . .
204. . . .
205. . . .

---

206. cherries* Patty*
207. . . .
208. . . .
209. . . .

---

210. . . .
211. geese* free*
212. magic* princess*
213. . . .
214. . . .
215. . . .
216. . . .

---

217. laugh-ingest* between*
218. . . .
219. hall*
220. . . .
221. . . .
222. . . .
223. . . .

---

224. (*Poem*)

UNIT VI

225. . . .
226. Freddy*
227. . . .
228. frog* wand*
229. . . .
230. . . .
231. . . .
232. . . .
233. . . .

---

234. . . .
235. . . .
236. win*
237. . . .
238. . . .

---

239. Milly* Flossy*
240. bug*
241. . . .
242. . . .
243. . . .
244. begins*
245. . . .
246. . . .

---

247. . . .
248. . . .
249. . . .
250. . . .
251. . . .
252. . . .

---

253. (*Poem*)

CDEFGHIJK 06987654

PRINTED IN THE UNITED STATES OF AMERICA